THE LAKE DISTRICT

Text by Terry Marsh · Photographs by Jon Sparks

SERIES EDITOR **Roly Smith**

PEVENSEY GUIDES

The Pevensey Press is an imprint of
David & Charles

First published in the UK in 2000

Map artwork by Chartwell Illustrators

Text copyright © Terry Marsh 2000
Photographs copyright © Jon Sparks 2000

Terry Marsh has asserted his right to be
identified as author of this work in
accordance with the Copyright, Designs
and Patents Act, 1988.

A catalogue record for this book is
available from the British Library.

ISBN 1 898630 11 9 (paperback)
ISBN 1 898630 23 2 (hardback)

Book design by
Les Dominey Design Company, Exeter
and printed in China by
Hong Kong Graphic & Printing Limited
for David & Charles
Brunel House   Newton Abbot   Devon

Contents

Page 1: Superb waterfall in Dungeon Ghyll, Langdale
Pages 2–3: The symbolic landscape of Wasdale
Left: Friar's Crag and across Derwent Water to Causey Pike

Front cover: (above) Great Langdale from Thrang Crag; (below) daffodils in Patterdale churchyard; (front flap) landing stages at Keswick, Derwent Water
Back cover: View over Windermere from Rosthwaite Heights

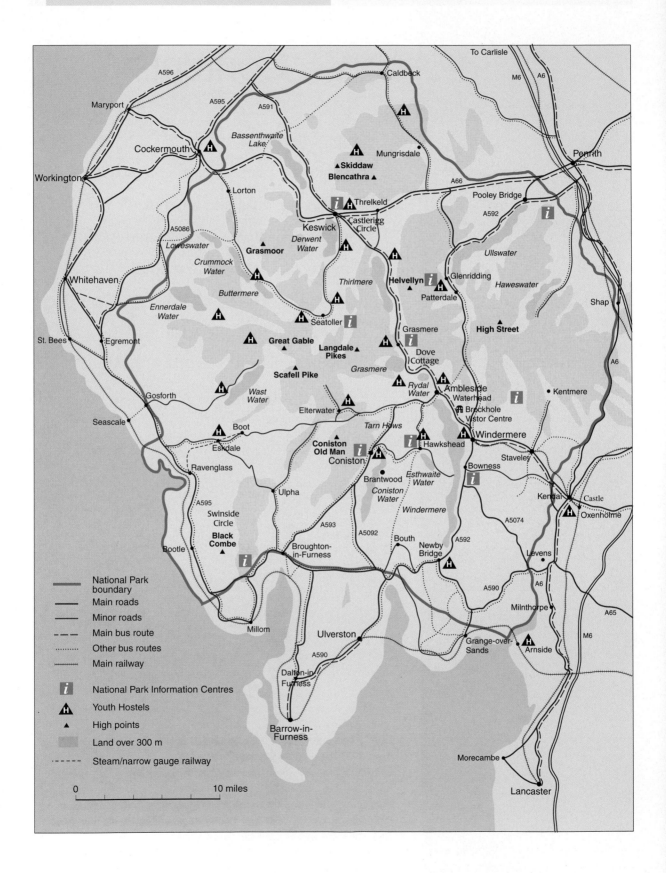

A596
A595
A591
To Carlisle
M6
A6
Maryport
Caldbeck
Cockermouth
Bassenthwaite Lake
Mungrisdale
Penrith
Workington
▲**Skiddaw**
Blencathra ▲
A66
Pooley Bridge
Lorton
i Threlkeld
A592
i
Keswick
Castlerigg Circle
A5086
Ullswater
Loweswater
Grasmoor ▲
Derwent Water
Whitehaven
Crummock Water
Thirlmere
Helvellyn *i*
Glenridding
Haweswater
Buttermere
▲ Patterdale
Shap
Ennerdale Water
▲ Seatoller
i
Grasmere *i*
High Street
St. Bees
Egremont
Great Gable
▲
Langdale Pikes ▲
Dove Cottage
A6
Scafell Pike ▲
Grasmere
Gosforth
Wast Water
Rydal Water
Ambleside
Waterhead
Kentmere
Seascale
Elterwater
Tarn Hows
Brockhole Vistor Centre
i
Boot
Coniston Old Man ▲
i
Hawkshead
Windermere
Eskdale
Coniston
Staveley
Ravenglass
Brantwood
Esthwaite Water
Bowness
i
Kendal
Castle
Ulpha
Coniston Water
Oxenholme
A595
Windermere
A5074
Swinside Circle
A593
A5092
Bouth
Newby Bridge
A592
Levens
Black Combe ▲
Broughton-in-Furness
i
A590
A6
Bootle
Milnthorpe
A65
Millom
M6
Ulverston
Grange-over-Sands
Arnside
A590
Dalton-in-Furness
Morecambe
Barrow-in-Furness
Lancaster

Legend

― National Park boundary
― Main roads
― Minor roads
--- Main bus route
······· Other bus routes
······· Main railway

i National Park Information Centres
H Youth Hostels
▲ High points
▨ Land over 300 m
- - - Steam/narrow gauge railway

0 ———————— 10 miles

Foreword

by Professor Ian Mercer CBE, Secretary General, Association of National Park Authorities

The National Parks of Great Britain are very special places. Their landscapes include the most remote and dramatic hills and coasts in England and Wales, as well as the wild wetlands of the Broads. They still support the farming communities which have fashioned their detail over the centuries. They form the highest rank of the protected areas which society put in place in 1949. So, 1999 saw the fiftieth anniversary of the founding legislation which, incidentally, provided for Areas of Outstanding Natural Beauty, Nature Reserves, Areas of Special Scientific Interest and Long Distance Footpaths, as well as for National Parks.

In the eight years following that, ten Parks were designated. The Lake District, the Peak, Snowdonia and Dartmoor were already well visited, as were the North York Moors, Pembrokeshire Coast, Yorkshire Dales and Exmoor which quickly followed. The Brecon Beacons and Northumberland had their devotees too, though perhaps in lesser numbers then. The special quality of each of these places was already well known, and while those involved may not have predicted the numbers, mobility or aspirations of visitors accurately, the foresight of the landscape protection system cannot be too highly praised.

That system has had to evolve – not just to accommodate visitor numbers, but to meet the pressures flowing from agricultural change, hunger for housing and roadstone, thirst for water, and military manoeuvring – and indeed, the Norfolk and Suffolk Broads were added to the list in 1989. National Parks are now cared for by free-standing authorities who control development, hold land, grant-aid farmers and others, provide wardens, information, car parks and loos, clear footpaths and litter, plant trees and partner many other agents in pursuit of the purposes for which National Parks exist. Those purposes are paramount for all public agencies' consideration when they act within the Parks. They are:

- the conservation of the natural beauty, wildlife and cultural heritage of the area, and
- the promotion of the understanding and enjoyment of its special qualities by the public.

The National Park Authorities must, in pursuing those purposes, foster social and economic well-being. They now bring in some £48 million a year between them to be deployed in the Parks, in addition to normal local public spending.

This book is first a celebration of the National Park, of all its special qualities and of the people whose predecessors produced and maintained the detail of its character. The series to which this book belongs celebrates too the first fifty years of National Park protection in the United Kingdom, the foresight of the founding fathers, and the contributions since of individuals like John Sandford, Reg Hookway and Ron Edwards. The book and the series also mark the work of the present National Park Authorities and their staff, at the beginning of the next fifty years, and of the third millennium of historic time. Their dedication to their Parks is only matched by their aspiration for the sustainable enhancement of the living landscapes for which they are responsible. They need, and hope for, your support.

In the new century, national assets will only be properly maintained if the national will to conserve them is made manifest to national governments. I hope this book will whet your appetite for the National Park, or help you get more from your visit, and provoke you to use your democratic influence on its behalf. In any case it will remind you of the glories of one of the jewels in Britain's landscape crown. Do enjoy it.

Introducing the Lake District

Twelve million people can't be wrong: that's how many visitors there are to the Lake District each year, vastly swamping the resident population of 42,000. The region attracts visitors from all over the world.

They are attracted by the outstanding quality of the landscape and the grandeur of the scenery. And by the very act of visiting the region, they serve to echo William Wordsworth's vision, expressed in his (1810) *Guide to the Lakes*, of a 'sort of national property, in which every man has a right and interest who has an eye to perceive and a heart to enjoy'.

Traditionally, it is Wordsworth and the so-called 'Lake Poets' who are said to have popularised the Lake District. But the prominence of the region evolved just as much from the coincidence of a number of differing circumstances and influences, beginning with the development of the nation's road network. This began in the aftermath of the 1745 Jacobite Rebellion which had highlighted the need to improve communications between England and Scotland. By 1768, the main route through what was then Westmorland and Cumberland – now the A591 – was in place. It meant that for at least one central stretch – from Kendal to Keswick – the erstwhile boggy, pot-holed tracks and trails had been replaced by a surfaced road accessible by private carriages.

Opposite: Landuse patterns in Longsleddale, seen from Buckbarrow

Overleaf: Winter morning. Low Peel Near, Coniston Water

Below: Cottages at Ravenglass, and Black Combe

Coincidental with this, many of the educated English gentry were beginning to acquire an interest in landscapes that were, to use a hackneyed word, picturesque. Paradoxically, it was the Grand Tour of Europe that was instrumental in developing this interest, as British landscape painters, influenced by Italian and French artists, started to search the further reaches of England for their inspiration. The dramatic scenery of the Lake District, full of mountain images, lakes and waterfalls, was reminiscent of the work of European painters, and exactly what English artists were looking for.

But the notion of the Lake District as a region with its own identity was first aroused by the poet Thomas Gray, who travelled through the Lakes in 1769. Viewing the landscape as a work of art, Gray described it vividly in numerous letters to his friend, Thomas Wharton. Within two years, Gray had died, and, in 1775, his letters were published by another friend, William Mason, also a poet.

Inspired by Gray's letters, Thomas West, a topographer and Jesuit mission-priest, first published his *Guide to the Lakes* in 1778. It was dedicated to 'Lovers of Landscape Studies and to all who have Visited, or Intend to visit the Lakes in Cumberland, Westmorland and Lancashire'. This was the first real tourist guidebook to the Lake District (as distinct from personal accounts), and described the vantage points from which the best views could be obtained.

By the time revolution and war rendered European travel unsafe, notably in the 1790s, the middle and upper classes were looking northward for their recreation, and travelling in the Lake District can be said truly to have begun. From that day, guidebooks flowed ceaselessly from the presses, and have scarcely abated ever since.

Although born in Cumberland – at Cockermouth – it was not until they were in their twenties that William and Dorothy Wordsworth decided to make the Lake District their home. They came to live in Grasmere in 1799 and never again lived away from the Lakes, and only moved the short distance from Grasmere to Rydal. And although William's presence attracted Coleridge and de Quincey, and later Southey, who was drawn to the Lakes by Coleridge, their grouping as the 'Lake Poets' was more a literary simplification than an indicator of a true coterie of like-minded individuals; in reality they had little in common, except an interest in the landscape.

Top: The interior of St Olaf's, Wasdale Head
Above: A corner of Boot village, Eskdale

Wordsworth's reputation grew, and during Victorian times in particular, his philosophical reflections in *The Excursion* had widespread impact, but most notably perhaps on the young John Ruskin who, after numerous visits to the Lakes, finally settled at Brantwood, overlooking Coniston Water, in 1872. Ruskin, like Wordsworth, attracted many friends to the Lakes, including one young admirer, Hardwicke Drummond Rawnsley, who with others founded the National Trust, now the largest private landowner in the Lake District.

And it was Ruskin's private secretary, the English artist and archaeologist, William Gershom Collingwood (1854–1932), who did much to transform the historical and archaeological knowledge of the Lake District, and, by befriending a young author, Arthur Ransome, inadvertently helped to further popularise the region. Ransome, of course, went on to write children's novels, notably *Swallows and Amazons* (which appeared in 1930, and is set around Coniston and

Windermere), that were threaded with the subliminal message that the outdoors was a place of fun and adventure, where young people could also acquire skills that would help them in later life.

Spinning gallery at Hartsop

From these coincidences and associations then the popularity of the Lake District grew. Industry – mining, iron smelting, slate quarrying and charcoal production – played its part, too, but in a rather different way. Specifically, it was the way the mill towns and villages changed for their power from water to steam. Had the development of steam power not been quite so speedy as it was, there is the real possibility that the abundance of water would have overcome the major disadvantages – mainly remoteness and ruggedness of the terrain – and the Lake District might have become even more highly industrialised.

Strangely, in spite of its name, the Lake District has only one 'lake', Bassenthwaite; all the others are 'tarns', 'meres' or 'waters', though sixteen of

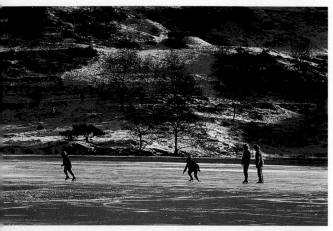

*Top: Tarn Hows: a winter playground
Above: Just after sunset: Haystacks
and High Stile ridge from Moses'
Trod*

Opposite: Sailing on Windermere

them fall within the conventional understanding of a lake. Indeed, Windermere is England's longest lake (17km/10½ miles from Waterhead to Lakeside) and Wastwater its deepest (79m/258ft). Three of them – Haweswater, Thirlmere and Ennerdale – have been enlarged to supply water to much of north west England.

It is this presence of so much water in such a compact area, set among dramatic fells and beautiful dales, that makes the Lake District different from any other part of Britain. Each lake is different, in size and shape, in its lakeside characteristics, in its wildlife, and in the extent to which it is available for recreational use.

But the lakes are only one ingredient among the many that make the landscape quality of Lakeland what it is: the fells, which, in Scafell Pike, include England's highest, the valleys or dales, and the towns and villages – almost 400 of them – all contribute to satisfy the vision of John Dower, whose report, published in 1945, augured the development of National Parks as extensive areas of 'beautiful and relatively wild country which should be preserved for the benefit of the nation'.

And it is this diversity that is the overwhelming feature of the district, noted as long ago as the sixteenth century by William Camden, who observed that it 'smileth upon the beholders and giveth contentment to as many as travaile it'. This is a place of contrasts and harmonies, of conflicts and tranquillity, of darkness and light, that together produce a synergy of happy balances, a whole that is far, far greater than the sum of its numerous parts.

This is a place of extremes, for not only does the Lake District boast the longest and deepest lakes in England and its highest mountains, but here, too, you'll find the steepest roads (Hardknott Pass is 33 per cent, or 1 in 3; Kirkstone and Honister are both 25 per cent, or 1 in 4). St Olaf's Church in Wasdale is claimed to be the smallest church in England. In Mardale, you may see England's only golden eagles and at Santon Bridge, listen to the World's Biggest Liar.

But the real beauty of the Lake District is change. There is constant change, from that which Nature herself imposes on the landscape – the geological tinkering that only time can trace; the variations on a theme composed by fluctuations in water flow; the fleeting, flattering fantasy of light that illuminates the fellsides and the fields of bright green solitude; the breath of wind across the still waters of a lake – to those that man himself adds to, or removes from, the scene.

The real beauty is change, combined with an inexplicable quality that brings so many visitors, whatever the weather, to spend a few hours or days in the most delectable of company; it is an addiction that is difficult to explain, but plain for all to see.

But at times change may need to be resisted, not all change is good. The landscape needs protection, and that is where the concept of a National Park comes in, although there is an essential theme that National Parks are also about the ability to enjoy what is within the park.

The Lake District National Park was created under the provisions of the

Studying the view from Whiteless Pike: Buttermere and the High Stile ridge

Top: Many Lakeland streams, like this at Boot, were used to power watermills

Above: Peacock butterfly on primroses

National Parks and Access to the Countryside Act 1949, and came into being on 15 August 1951. It is now managed by the National Park Authority which was set up under the Environment Act 1995 and took over the running of the Park in April 1997.

Covering 885 square miles (2,292 square kilometres), the Lake District National Park is the largest and most spectacular of Britain's National Parks, and vies with the Peak District for the distinction of being the most-visited of Britain's eleven National Parks. The boundary of the National Park has not changed since it was established in 1951. It encloses one third of the county of Cumbria, and extends from Caldbeck in the north to Lindale in the south, from Ravenglass in the west to Shap in the east.

The primary purposes of National Parks are given in the foreword to this book and in carrying these out the Lake District National Park Authority has a duty to foster the social and economic well-being of the local community.

To meet these obligations, the National Park Authority employs over 130 full-time permanent staff plus 60 seasonal staff (full- and part-time). In addition, there are over 240 active voluntary wardens and 80 probationary or honorary voluntary wardens.

So, apart from the obvious threat of unsuitable development, what does the Lake District need to be protected from? Simple – people!

The landscape of the Lake District is unquestionably beautiful and spectacular, and most people want to keep it that way. So careful thought needs to be given to anything that may alter the character of the landscape, and that doesn't just mean buildings. The Lake District is far more than the scattered man-made settlements, though, it has to be said, virtually all of it has been subjected to the influence of man one way or another since his first arrival.

If you could take a bird's-eye view of the Lake District you would see it all – the towns and villages, the fells and dales, the lakes and rivers, forests and large tracts of open ground. When we talk of change, the tendency is to think of changes in the valleys and the settlements, but the rest of the Lake District does not escape the hand (or foot) of change. Walkers and climbers wear away the paths, vegetation is destroyed, nesting birds can be disturbed, watercourses can become polluted. Farming, too, plays a part in this change. Sheep put out on the upper fells to graze not only keep the grass short, but eat other vegetation, including young saplings. If this didn't happen, the saplings would flourish and the Lake District would gradually revert to the vast forest it once was.

Today, although large areas are still wooded, the woodlands of the Lake District are nothing like as dense or widespread as they were before man arrived.

Above: Ravenglass and Eskdale Railway, near Eskdale Green

Below: Typical dry-stone wall, Combe Gill, Borrowdale

Here there is a fine mix of semi-natural broadleaved woodlands and totally coniferous plantations, the majority owned by the Forestry Commission. A total of 75,000 tonnes of timber are produced each year from Lakeland forests, and the forests themselves visited by over a million people.

From a different point of view, and of immense importance both in terms of management, conservation and as visitor attractions, there are over 200 scheduled ancient monuments in the Lake District dating from prehistoric times to the industrial period, including such places as the Castlerigg Stone Circle, Shap Abbey and the Roman remains at Ravenglass. Some are on private land, many are owned and managed by the National Trust, English Heritage, others are looked after by the National Park Authority.

Add to that 1,731 listed buildings and churches, eight National Nature Reserves, 120 Sites of Special Scientific Interest, and 82 Regionally Important Geological/Geomorphological Sites, and you begin to see not only what a special place the Lake District is in terms of Britain's heritage and conservation interests, but what a massive responsibility it is to manage it all, and to conserve it for posterity.

Above: Interior of the old church at Martindale
Left: Blea Tarn and the Langdale Pikes from Hawk Rigg

Overleaf: Derwent Water from Skiddaw

Contrary to what you might think, National Parks are not areas owned by the nation. The Lake District National Park owns only 3.8 per cent (8,600ha) of land. By far the largest land ownership is private, with 58.7 per cent (133,700ha).

The National Trust bought its first holding in 1902, thanks to gifts from Beatrix Potter, the historian G.M. Trevelyan, Sir Samuel Scott and others. Apart from the numerous farms it owns, most of its holdings are open to the public, and include large tracts of open fell.

North West Water has the next largest land ownership with 6 per cent (13,700ha), mainly in the Ennerdale, Thirlmere and Haweswater catchment areas. Until recent times, access to the company's land holdings was prohibited, but now you can wander freely around the shores of all these reservoirs, and even sail on Thirlmere.

Third in size of ownership is the Forestry Commission, which controls 5.6 per cent (12,700ha), and generally allows – and in many places actively encourages – free public access to its holdings.

It is access to the open countryside, however, that brings most visitors to Lakeland. The more energetic seek out the fells and the lakes; the more sedentary can do the same from a distance, or enjoy leisurely tours on foot, by car, or from one of the many organised sight-seeing tours that are available during the summer months.

But however you come to enjoy the Lakes, there is the certainty that even in those most popular of places there can still be, even for the most experienced explorer of the region, the joy of discovery and the peace of solitude.

1 The rocks beneath: geology and scenery

People come to the Lake District for a miscellany of reasons, among them, certainly, to see the scenery, the mountains (or 'fells' as they are known), and the lakes. Yet such a simplistic approach – not that there's anything wrong with it – is a case of not seeing the wood for the trees, or rather (since this section deals with geology) of not seeing the rocks for the mountains.

Yet, evidence of the geology of the Lake District is plainly there for everyone to see. Even the most cursory observation will show that the mountains are more than mere bumps in the landscape or the background to an attractive picture: they have a history, one that stretches our comprehension of time, into aeons past.

The landscape is full of crags, rocky knolls, and moulded fells that each betray the ancient underlying rocks. Everywhere you find examples of how the landscape was tailored by the agents of erosion, from deeply gouged glaciated valleys to weathered peaks. Also widespread is the trail of man's exploitation of the mineral wealth of the region, in scores of abandoned mines and quarries. And the whole landscape is spread with a mantle of dry-stone walls enclosing pastures and lanes, linking farms and villages, and all built with local stone, the rocks of Lakeland.

Rocks from three geological periods make up most of the Lake District, while other periods are well represented around the edges of the National Park. The laying down of two great sedimentary groups of rocks – Skiddaw Slates and Silurian rocks – is separated by a period during which the rocks of the Borrowdale Volcanic series appeared.

And it is a tempting misconception that the mountains must be composed of harder rocks than those forming the lower land. Because the region has been subjected to three major orogenic periods, plus recurrent faulting, the effect has been to place side-by-side rocks that were formed millions of years apart.

Each of the three major rock divisions produces its own distinctive scenery, and it is because you can often sit on one type of rock and conveniently compare its landscape with a completely different rock just across the valley (as in Buttermere, for example), that the study of Lakeland geology is so interesting. It helps, however, to

Great Gable – classic BVS rock scenery. Napes Crags can be seen just below the summit

THE ENGLISH ALPS

To see the mountains for themselves, to study their composition, to attempt to understand the processes and periods involved in creating this fabulous landscape, is both fascinating and rewarding. And adds immeasurably to a visit.

Nor is it an enormous undertaking, for the great beauty of the Lake District is its very compactness, so neat that it may well fit into Rannoch Moor in Scotland, and yet showing such remarkable diversity. Wordsworth compared the landscape of the Lake District – smooth and harmonious – with that of the Alps, which he felt suggested chaos. What influenced the comparison is the scale of things, for while the Alpine landscape is vast, in the Lake District the geology is much more concentrated.

In simple terms, the processes that made the Lake District fall into three distinct, but overlapping, times: periods of deposition and volcanic activity, during which the rocks were formed; a time of mountain building, what the geologists call orogenesis, and a period of denudation, when the landscape was worn away.

Ennerdale granophyre on the shores of Ennerdale Water

have some basic understanding of the rock types, of which there are three main groups – *sedimentary, igneous* and *metamorphic*.

Sedimentary rocks were formed as mud settling under water or on land. The sediments were later subjected to immense pressure, which hardened them into rocks many thousand metres thick. The component materials of these sediments, however, have three categories: *clastic*, eg bits of pre-existing rocks; *organic*, eg plant or animal remains; or *inorganic*, eg produced by chemical action. It is not unusual, however, to find rock composed of a mix of these materials, containing both quartz grains (clastic) and fossils (organic).

Igneous rocks, as the name suggests, have something to do with fire, and originate in massive reservoirs of liquid material, called *magma*, within the upper mantle of the earth. Along weaknesses in the earth's crust, magma can force a way through, following which it cools and solidifies. If this cooling takes place within the crust, the rocks are called *intrusive*; if it occurs once the magma has broken through the surface, the rocks are known as *extrusive*.

Finally, metamorphic rocks are those which have in some way changed their characteristics as a result of heat or pressure. Either of the two other types of rock can become metamorphosed over lengthy periods of time, and may involve only slight changes, ie low-grade metamorphism, or complete reconstitution, ie high-grade metamorphism.

South of the Skiddaw Slates lie the rocks of the Borrowdale Volcanic Series (BVS), which were formed during the late Ordovician period. These rocks form a broad band across the National Park from the boundary in the east along the River Lowther, along a line that touches upon the northern edge of Windermere and Coniston Water, to Black Combe in the south-west.

The BVS rocks support the highest and most rugged part of Lakeland, the central massif, wild, dark and craggy, with extensive downfalls of boulders and scree, and includes the popular peaks of Scafell Pike, its neighbour, Scafell, and the more distant fells of Helvellyn, Fairfield, Great Gable, the Langdale Pikes and the Old Man of Coniston. This very ruggedness attracts walkers and rock climbers alike.

It was during Ordovician times that the landscape was rent apart by massive volcanic eruptions which spilled lava from the bowels of the earth to form huge accumulations of material from fine ashes and dust – tuffs – to large rocks that later solidified into bouldery masses – agglomerates. The rocky upthrust of Castle Head in Borrowdale is said to be a plug in one of the many volcanic vents spread across the landscape, mainly in the west.

After the volcanoes fell silent, the region was uplifted to form a mountainous land mass, and subjected to millions of years of erosion before shallow seas again encroached and deposited another series of clastic and organic sediments that consolidated to form the Coniston Limestone Group. Very little can be seen of this group because most of it was later eroded and much of what remained was overlaid. But a strip of it can be found running across the southern slopes of the Old Man of Coniston and through Tarn Hows and the top end of Windermere. Tarn Hows, an immensely popular beauty spot, is a perfect place from which to contrast the rocks of this group and the Borrowdale Volcanics in the distance.

Those botanically inclined may spot the floral difference here between plants that favour lime and those that prefer the surrounding acidic conditions; abandoned lime kilns are also a key clue.

Further south, is another region of slates and siltstones, the upper of the two great sedimentary groups. These, too, were formed as marine sediments, but here during

Silurian times, about 440–400 million years ago. Geologists know these rocks as the Windermere Group, and the main concentration of them provides the delectable landscape that lies either side of the main access route from the south (the A591). The Windermere Group is much less resistant than the BVS rocks, and produce in consequence a delightful range of modest fells stretching from the Duddon Estuary to Kendal, just outside the National Park boundary (but the location of the authority's headquarters). The scenery around Coniston and Windermere is typically formed from these rocks, and produces a soft, rounded country, often wooded. Lovely Esthwaite Water, the Furness Fells and the Winster Valley are also part of this lush and verdant landscape.

Beginning about 350 million years ago, the land gradually sank beneath a tropical sea as the earth entered the Carboniferous Period. The notion that the Lake District we know may once have formed part of a 'tropical' sea may seem odd, but the land mass at these distant times was much further south than now. Since the formation of the Skiddaw Slates the earth's crust has slowly been drifting northwards, but it began from a position well south of the equator. By about 250 million years ago, it had reached a latitude equivalent to the present day Sahara Desert.

The Carboniferous sea was full of primitive life forms, corals, molluscs and stone-lilies (crinoids), which, as they died, produced a thick sediment of shells which

Top: Glaciated landscape: Mickleden, at the head of Great Langdale
Above: Dry-stone walls on Claife Heights

SKIDDAW SLATE

It was during Ordovician times (500–440 million years ago), when the land mass that included the Britain of today was submerged beneath a shallow sea, that the oldest rocks in the Lake District – known as Skiddaw Slates – were formed. These are mostly dark, fine-grained, clastic sedimentary rocks, but unlike the 'slates' normally associated with roofing materials, Skiddaw Slates have minute fractures within them, which causes them to fragment easily and produce an overall scenic impression of smoothness and rolling fellsides, free of sharp-profiled crags, typified in particular by the unbroken outline of Skiddaw itself. Most of these rocks are found north of a line from Ennerdale Water, past Derwent Water towards the eastern boundary of the National Park.

The most notable examples of Skiddaw Slates are, of course, the northern fells, including the massive summits of Skiddaw itself, its neighbour Blencathra, and most of the fells in the area traditionally known as 'Back o'Skidda'. You can see the characteristics most notably from the top of Carrock Fell, north of Mungrisdale, from which flows a seemingly endless series of smooth-topped fells and soft-sided valleys. Carrock Fell is of particular importance in this example, since it is quite evidently not of Skiddaw Slates. The summit bears the remains of a hill-fort of uncertain age, but quite clearly made of completely alien rocks: it is in fact a separate and very localised example of an igneous intrusion, ie magma rocks formed within the earth's crust, but later exposed by earth movements or weathering.

Elsewhere in the Lake District, the Skiddaw Slates have been overlaid with other material, but they outcrop again at the southern extreme in Black Combe, a massive whaleback of a mountain and conspicuously visible from far out to sea and from the distant moorlands of Lancashire. Other prominent fells that are composed of Skiddaw Slates are the graceful Grisedale Pike and Causey Pike. From the top of Dale Head above Honister Pass, you can compare the distinct, soft profile of the Skiddaw Slate·fells to the north with the more dramatic and craggy fells in central Lakeland to the south, that are fashioned from a quite different material.

compressed into what we know today as limestone. But gradually the sea was filled in with mud and sand, which was then colonised by swampy forests, the remains of which today form coal. There is supposition that there was a time when the whole of the Lake District was covered by these fossil deposits, but today they only exist around the edges, and largely outside the National Park boundary.

About 280 million years ago, the relatively quiet period of Carboniferous times ended and we enter the Permo-Triassic period when the Carboniferous rocks were uplifted by the Hercynian Orogeny, the second episode of mountain building. This was a rather less intense period of upheaval than its predecessor, but one which raised the old rocks into a rough dome shape, opened old faults, created new ones, and then suffered erosion on a grand scale. Inexorably, this removed the Carboniferous limestone cover, and all that remained was a girdle around the central high mountains, notably on the northern edge of the National Park and along the south, where it is only partly within the Park: Whitbarrow Scar and Scout Scar are prime examples.

It is from this time that Coniston's copper and the lead that was mined in Glenridding originate. But while this period is generally accepted for copper and lead, there is rather more uncertainty about precisely when many of the other minerals were formed.

The Lake District, of course, is famous for its lakes. They and their rivers radiate like the spokes of a wheel from a central point in a pattern familiar to all students of Lakeland geology and geography. But quite how this came about is not as clear-cut as you might expect, since what happened in the Post-Triassic period (195–192 million years ago), is unclear. It has been suggested that there was a further advance of the sea during Cretaceous times (135 million years ago), with the resultant sedimentation. This was then uplifted during the Alpine Orogeny (135–70 million years ago), the third phase of mountain building, and the same event that produced the Alps, the Rockies and the Himalaya. Slowly and intermittently, it lifted the British Isles, still part of the Continent, out of the sea, doming the central area around the Scafells. It was upon this broad dome that the radial drainage pattern was superimposed, exploiting faults within the hard rocks and cutting through the softer ones.

Thereafter, for many more millions of years, the land was eroded mainly by weathering, though there were still a few earth movements, but nothing on the scale of before. This state persisted until about two millions years ago, when the earth's climate cooled and ice sheets spread across Britain during what is generally known as the Pleistocene Glaciation. Summers were cool and so the winter snows never melted, becoming consolidated into vast ice fields that covered much of the northern hemisphere. In the Lake District, only the highest peaks, by this time at something like their present height, would have been clear of the ice.

There were a number of advances and retreats, each leaving behind a trail of erosion and sculpting, though it is not easy to determine how much impact each advance had on the landscape. It was only in the last 20,000 years that the permanent ice fields finally left Britain. Mini-glaciation continued, however, until the end of the last Ice Age, about 11,000 years ago. It is the action of this last period, a further period of glaciers and meltwater, frost and tundral conditions, that put the final touches, as we shall know them, to the landscape.

But it is far from over. We are now living in a slightly warmer period known as an interglacial, which suggests that the Ice Age has not yet ended. If another glacial period began it would start in the high, east- and north-facing corries of the Lake District where, even now, after severe winters accumulations of snow still linger well into summer.

At its greatest extent, the ice flowed out from the central region along existing river valleys, east towards the Vale of Eden, the Tyne Gap and the Stainmore Gap; north around the Caldbeck Fells, where it met and was deflected by Scottish ice

Above: Glacial striations above Church Beck, Coniston
Opposite: Slate slabs in a wall near Hawkshead

Below: Carboniferous limestone on the south-east aspect of Whitbarrow Scar

COLLIDING CONTINENTS

After the Silurian interlude there followed a convulsive period known as the Caledonian Orogeny, the sort of event that arises from the collision of two continents, as typified by the Himalaya. This occurred during the Devonian period, about 400–350 million years ago, a turbulent time during which arid conditions prevailed and all the rocks were repeatedly folded, faulted, intruded by magma, and generally pushed about on a grand scale. It was during this period that many of the fine lava ashes, the tuffs, were compressed to form the beautiful and much-sought after Westmorland green slate. And it was at this time that the familiar ENE–WSW trend lines of Lakeland geology were set.

That little visible remains of this geologically traumatic episode is due to millions of years of erosion, although there are still many folds and faults for us to see today, albeit in a picture of considerable complexity. At the same time as this cataclysmic disturbance, there was a massive spread of igneous intrusions – cooling magma forced into the fractures within the earth's crust. Where this occurred, the pre-existing rocks were changed (metamorphosed) chemically and physically, and a good deal of the mineral wealth on which, much later, the Lakeland economy was founded for many years, comes from this period.

Buttermere and Crummock Water, once a single lake

flows, west into the Irish Sea ice; west along the course of Buttermere, Ennerdale and Wasdale; and south via Coniston and Windermere into Morecambe Bay.

When we look at the Lakeland landscape today, we see more than anything else the handiwork of glaciers. As the glacier moved along it scoured the rocks beneath, sculpting them by the combined action of its own incredible weight and the force it applies to rock debris carried along by it. It literally bulldozed its way through the valleys, making them deeper and, where they were V-shaped (fashioned by rivers), made them the distinctive U-shape associated with glaciation. The valley ice, being of greater volume and weight, ploughed its way onwards, cutting off many lesser tributary valleys, and so creating what are known as 'hanging' valleys. You can see examples of these today at the head of Swindale, where Mosedale Beck now enters the main valley in steep waterfalls, and in Borrowdale, at Seathwaite, above which Gillercomb is superb. It was in the valleys that were deepened the most by this glacial action that, when the ice retreated, the lakes were formed.

The final act of the Pleistocene Glaciation saw glaciers clinging to the high mountain corries, persisting in deeply shaded hollows. When at last they went they left a superb legacy of mountain tarns, reached only by hill walkers, and as worthy an objective of a day out in the fells as any summit might be. They are distinctive and delightful, and most are well known: Bowscale Fell and Scales Tarn in the northern fells; Blea Water and Small Water above the end of Mardale; Angle Tarn and Stickle Tarn in the central fells; Red Tarn below Helvellyn, and Bleaberry Tarn near High Pike.

Occasionally, the mountain corries form on both sides of a fell, gradually widening so that they create a narrow crest, or arête, between them. The two classic

Above: Screes at Wastwater

Opposite: (top) Small Water, a classic example of a mountain tarn; (below) The head of Borrowdale from Watendlath Fell

HANGING VALLEYS

The hanging valleys are a stunning feature of the Lakeland landscape. From them water spills in steep cascades and after rain provides a breathtaking sight. There are many of these waterfalls, and everyone has a favourite. Sour Milk Gill below Red Pike in Buttermere, perhaps, or Taylorgill Force and the Falls of Lodore in Borrowdale, Dungeon Ghyll in Langdale, or Stock Ghyll near Ambleside.

examples, of course, are Striding Edge, which rises between Red Tarn Cove and Nethermost Cove, and Swirral Edge, between Red Tarn Cove and Brown Cove. But there is another in Sharp Edge on Blencathra.

But it doesn't all end there for after the last period of glaciation the region was washed by storms and floods, which scoured the barren landscape and swept tons of silt and debris into the lakes creating, over a long period of time, two lakes where previously there was one, or even silting up lakes altogether. From the top of High Pike you can easily see how Buttermere and Crummock Water were once a single lake, and from Latrigg above Keswick, how Derwent Water and Bassenthwaite Lake would once have been combined. Less certain is the notion that Langdale may have once held a lake, but in the mysterious and fascinating world of geology all things seem possible; they just have to be proven.

Finally, it is not surprising that the wide range of valuable mineral deposits has been exploited. In the sixteenth century, the Lake District was Britain's chief producer of copper, and the principal source of haematite 300 years later. Between these times, Borrowdale yielded a unique deposit of graphite, which saw the foundation of Keswick's famous pencil manufacturing industry. Wolfram was mined from the depths of Carrock, the only place outside Devon and Cornwall to prove commercially viable. Other sites have produced lead, zinc, manganese, cobalt, nickel and barytes.

There is a twelfth-century mention of an iron mine at Egremont, just outside the National Park, and such was the quantity of copper in the Goldscope Mines near Keswick that Elizabeth I brought in German miners, and set up the Company of Mines Royal. This endeavour soon made the Lake District the most important centre in Britain for smelting copper-lead-silver ores.

Graphite and iron ore mining continued to flourish during the seventeenth century, extracting large quantities from veins in the Borrowdale Volcanic Series of the Central Fells. By the end of the century, however, copper mining was in decline, and the mines in Newlands and at Caldbeck were almost exhausted, though the mines at Coniston continued until a slump in copper prices in 1895 forced a closure. The Greenside Mine, near Helvellyn, yielded an important deposit of lead, first discovered in the 1650s, and which far exceeded the total for the rest of the Lake District before it, too, closed in the 1960s.

Mineral production is today significantly less than it was, and primarily concerned with the quarrying of slate, stone and aggregates. There are three important slate quarries currently operating in Elterwater, Broughton Moor and Kirkstone, along with others at Coniston and at other small sites that work intermittently, as demand for their particular slate requires.

There are two major granite quarries at Shap, and limestone quarries straddling the boundary at Kendal Fell and Shap.

Striding Edge in winter, with the corrie lake of Red Tarn beyond

2 Climate, vegetation and wildlife

*Above: Moss and lichen, Ennerdale
Below: Ice formations in Small
Water Beck in winter*

*Opposite: Ancient semi-natural
woodlands (mostly oak), Troutdale*

Cumbria, embracing the entire Lake District National Park, has a cool oceanic climate, but one so remarkable that it has the widest climatic diversity of any English county. Throughout the northern counties, however, there is a common saying that we don't have 'climate', we just have 'weather'.

Sadly, there seems to be a morbid pre-occupation with rainfall. And yet the number of rainy days in the Lake District, excluding the high summits, is little different from most other parts of England.

What tends to bitter the pill is the fact that the area around the central fells is indisputably the wettest place in Britain, with an average annual rainfall of 172in (439cm); nearby Seathwaite is Britain's wettest inhabited spot, with an average rainfall of 140in (325cm). But away from the effects of the mountains, the rainfall is significantly less, almost sixty per cent less in Ambleside, for example.

Basically, the climate of the Lake District is that of a small, compact group of mountains and valleys to leeward of a wide expanse of ocean that is uncharacteristically warm for its latitude, which almost corresponds with Moscow. It is the Atlantic air currents and the effects of the Gulf Stream that dominate the Lake District climate, and that means fairly mild winter temperatures, but rather cooler summers. And though the amount and extent of snow cover may not compare with Scotland's mountains, certainly if your interest is skiing, snow does linger in many of the sheltered, north-east facing coombes well into June and July.

COME RAIN OR SHINE

The Lakeland climate should not deter you from exploring the district. A holiday anywhere in Britain is a chance thing weather-wise, and the Lake District is no exception. The secret is to come well equipped, so that the weather makes no difference; expect rain and cold, and anything else is a bonus. It is, after all, on your own way of coping with all things, not only the weather, that the success and pleasure of your stay will depend. But, as Wordsworth observed in his Guide to the Lakes *'the showers, darkening, or brightening, as they fly from hill to hill, are not less grateful to the eye than finely interwoven passages of gay and sad music are touching to the ear'. He had much to say about clouds, too, which were 'pregnant with imagination lifting up suddenly their glittering heads from behind rocky barriers, or hurrying out of sight [tempting] an inhabitant to congratulate himself on belonging to a country of mists and clouds and storms, and make him think of the blank sky of Egypt, and of the cerulean vacancy of Italy, as an unanimated and even a sad spectacle.'*

Ask any landscape photographer whether they prefer clear skies or stormy light, and without exception it will be the latter, for then it is that you catch the magical moment when sunlight bursts through the clouds that in turn cast restless shadows across the fellsides, driven by implacable breezes that ripple the vibrant colours of fell and forest, and inject movement and excitement into waterfalls, lakes and streams alike. Unquestionably, there is immense pleasure in bright, leg-swinging days on the fells, warmed by sunshine and able to see forever. But there is something spellbinding, too, about a sudden clearing in the mists that reveals a whole new landscape, beckoning like an impatient child.

Not long ago, I walked from Shap to Keld and into the beautiful, glaciated valley of Swindale, over Mosedale and back through Wet Sleddale. On that day – it was early February – the sky was filled with the dark, mobile furniture of storm clouds that alternately sent down ice-edged squalls of rain and produced shadow-flecked sunlit expanses of valley and moorland. High up in Mosedale I sat in the meagre shelter of a sheepfold and, disinclined to move on, ate lunch and let the whole gamut of Lakeland weather sweep over me in the space of an hour; it was a memorable hour – just me, wild moorland and the Lakeland weather.

But if the weather proves too much for you, there is always hospitality and a welcome in hundreds of country pubs, tea shops and visitor centres where a pot of tea and cream-laden scones can work wonders with the spirit.

Derwent Water and Causey Pike

Esthwaite Water, one of the most beautiful of lakeland tarns, with marginal reeds

The Lake District today contains an exceptionally rich diversity of habitat including mountain tops, broadleaved woodlands, peatlands, limestone pavements, lakes and tarns, estuaries and coast, each of which supports a wide range of plants and animals. When prehistoric man arrived in Lakeland about 6,000 years ago, however, it was vastly different. From isolated rocky knolls he would have looked out across a landscape dominated by woodland. But the woodland didn't spring up overnight, it was the product of thousands of years of painstaking work by nature.

At the end of the last glacial period, the soil was almost entirely mineral, what is known as skeletal soil. It had been scoured clean by massive grinding glaciers. Very little could grow in this barren landscape, because for trees and plants to thrive much more is needed. The necessary ingredients came from a gradual building up of organic matter and nitrogen produced by the growth of lichens and mosses, which were able to survive on the harsh soils. As the climate warmed, the lichens and mosses were supplemented by grasses and herbaceous plants, and then by the appearance of shrubs, like juniper and dwarf willow, which flourished as more stable soil conditions developed. On many of the high Lakeland summits you can still see this soil production happening where mats of lichen, sphagnum moss and hair-moss are building up humus in the form of dark, crumbly peat.

There is no way of knowing what kind of woodland would develop in the Lake District today if the influence of man and his animals was removed. It is doubtful that it would recreate that first Lakeland forest, because the climate and soils are possibly very different. Much has been learned, however, about the pioneer vegetation through the analysis of pollen from the shores of upland tarns and boggy hollows among glacial moraine.

If we could watch this evolution condensed into a few moments we would see birch quickly spreading across the landscape, but from about 7000BC giving way to hazel which then became dominant. Hazel, too, suffers a setback as its advance is slowed down by the expansion of oak and elm. The elm seeks out damp loamy conditions, while the oak steadily invades the areas dominated by birch and hazel. Pine, too, features in this early scene, colonising the lower ground, but being progressively banished to the upper fells as the broadleaved trees take over.

Today, it takes the power of such imagination to visualise this vast woodland cover, especially when all you have to go on are pollen grains preserved in peat. But there are a few places where the stumps and roots of ancient trees have been uncovered, and provide much more convincing proof. More than 2,000 feet up in Langdale, severe flooding and landslip, notably in 1962 following torrential rain, revealed the roots of Scots pine and some broadleaved trees. These, and other examples, can still be found high on the fells, and provide a glimpse into the woodland past of the region.

The pattern of vegetation in the Lake District is reflective of altitude. On the higher fells, heath and grassland predominates, while below, in the sub-montane zone, the grassland found is of varying quality.

The vegetation of any region is vitally important, of course, because it provides food and shelter for most other forms of wildlife. The natural boundaries of a region can usually be identified by the vegetation they contain. In the Lake District, there are five main regions, or zones: marine, agricultural, fell, mountain top and aquatic.

The marine coastline stretches for 12 miles (19km) from Drigg and Ravenglass to Silecroft on the western boundary of the National Park, and incorporates small parts of the Duddon Estuary and Morecambe Bay in the south. A brief tour of this area reveals the most extensive sand dune system in Cumbria and areas of coastal heath, grazing marshes and tidal reedbeds, invaluable habitats and many of national and international importance. And, over time you can see that the coastline itself is a place of constant change, as sand and silt are washed away with each tide, only to be replaced with the next.

The beaches, gently sloping, comprise patches of sand alternating with pebble and boulder beds. Among the latter, bladder wrack and toothed wrack are widespread, while above the limit of high spring tides the first flowering plants occur, notably curled dock, gorse, sea campion and red fescue.

In the Ravenglass Estuary and the small bit of Morecambe Bay that is within the Park there is a small area of saltmarsh, a region of fine mud along a gently sloping shoreline. At the seaward extreme, the mud is bare and colonised by isolated plants of glasswort. Channels through bare mud dissect the middle reaches of the marsh, but higher up the vegetation forms a complete cover.

At Ravenglass and Eskmeals there are extensive sand dunes, which, nearest the sea, still have highly mobile sand where marram grass and lyme grass grow, and this has the effect of stabilising the dunes. Inland from the dunes are shallow depressions, called slacks, often filled with water especially during winter, and exceptionally rich in flora such as creeping willow and marsh pennywort.

Goosey Foot Tarn, deep in Grizedale Forest

The Esk estuary at Ravenglass

Top: *Wood sorrel*
Above: *Meadowsweet and tufted vetch*

Right: *The brilliant green of young larch shoots*

Away from the coast you enter the agricultural zone, which can be loosely defined as the area below the open fellside, often delineated by a mountain wall, that is capable of being ploughed. It comprises a wide range of land from coastal plain to sheltered dales.

The low-lying areas are invariably poorly drained, resulting in the development of marshland. Unattractive as this may sound, it nevertheless produces an excellent habitat, especially where, as at Rusland, willows have spread onto the marshes, producing a scrubland that is ideal cover for a wide range of birdlife. At North Fen Nature Reserve to the north of Esthwaite Water there is a prime example of how marshland area and open water becomes colonised by vegetation. Flag iris and bottle sedge flourish here, while elsewhere alder shares the damp conditions with brooklime and water starwort.

Common throughout Lakeland are woodlands and plantations, which add enormously to the diversity of the landscape. They include two National Forest Parks, at Grizedale and Whinlatter, while the predominantly broadleaved semi-natural woodlands are recognised as one of the Lake District's most valuable scenic and wildlife assets.

Providing a tenuous link with ancient times, stands of sessile oak (recognisable by the absence of stalks on the acorns) in some dales, notably Borrowdale, and Keskadale and Birkrigg in Newlands, are thought by botanists to be the nearest extant examples of 'natural' woodland, descendants of the woodland that our pre-historic man gazed over.

Exquisitely beautiful mixed woods of oak, birch, hazel, alder, elm and ash, formerly managed as enclosed coppice and exploited for woodland industries, can be found throughout the Lake District, but most extensively between the Duddon and Windermere. Here, too, you will find small-leaved lime, once the most common tree in lowland England. There are splendid specimens on the limestone around Morecambe Bay and in southern Lakeland, some of considerable age, up to 2,300 years old.

Beneath the trees the ground cover varies with geology, drainage and light, and you can expect to find bluebells, wood anemones, primroses, foxgloves, wood sorrel, meadowsweet and wild garlic. Ash and hazel prefer limestone, and here the

ground cover may include dog's mercury, orchids and lily of the valley.

Among the trees themselves it is not uncommon to find all three native wood-peckers, though the lesser spotted, which is small and prefers the tree tops, is rather elusive. Wood warbler is also present along with chaffinch, redstart, robin, wren, members of the tit family and pied flycatcher, as well as the gymnastic tree creeper and nuthatch.

'Amenity' woodlands were developed and planted by landowners and are only distinguishable from the second type by the inclusion of larch and beech (not present before the eighteenth century) and a higher proportion of other alien trees, including pine and sycamore. Most of the woodlands in the Windermere–Ambleside–Grasmere corridor are of this type, and are found on many of the large estates. They attract many of the more familiar birds like blackbird, but are appreciated also by siskin and one of Britain's tiniest birds, the goldcrest.

One final type of woodland is completely non-native, and comes courtesy of the Forestry Commission and private landowners. Most of these 'plantations', a word that distinguishes them from native woodlands, contain European larch and Norway or Sitka spruce, and are there for primarily commercial reasons. They are relatively poor in flora and fauna.

Characteristic flora of a different kind is also associated with the hedgerows, which, in intensively farmed areas, are a vital refuge for all forms of wildlife, and often provide a clue to the sort of plants you could expect if the influence of man was not present. Take a stroll beside the hedgerows of the lowland areas and you are likely to find hazel, bramble, wild rose and ash, while on the nutrient-poor soils further north – the Skiddaw Slates and Borrowdale Volcanics – hawthorn is widespread. These harsher conditions also favour foxglove and wood sage, instead of the goose grass and red campion found in the lowlands. Where limestone occurs, look for wood geranium and field scabious, devil's-bit scabious and wood cranesbill, the latter a species that so epitomises early summer in the Lakes, but which has almost disappeared from its typical hay-meadow habitat because of excessive use of fertilisers and the change to silage.

Above the farms most of the land in the Lake District is open fell. This is the landscape most visitors have come to see. Here, as elsewhere, the vegetation is

Top: Red admiral on devil's-bit scabious
Above: Butterbur

Left: Whitebeam

TOUGH AT THE TOP

The mountain tops occupy as little as 5 per cent of the National Park, and provide the most hostile environment in which vegetation grows. Here plants can be frozen at night and burned by day, soaked by rain and mist, and blasted by winds. Vegetation displays characteristics common to Arctic conditions, growing slowly and consisting of long-lived perennials. Yet amazingly cowberry, Alpine clubmoss, wavy hair moss, lichens and liverworts all flourish. True Arctic plants – dwarf willow and stiff sedge – grow on the fells on the north side of Ennerdale, among the Coniston fells and on St Sunday Crag, and are fairly common above 550m.

Top: Sea campion
Above: Common butterwort
Right: Wind-blown yew on Whitbarrow Scar
Opposite: Ancient oak, with mosses and ferns, Rydal

determined by the underlying soil, but it is much less obviously disturbed by man than in the valleys. Rough grassland, comprising sheep's fescue and bent grass, is widespread and often invaded by bracken, beneath which you frequently encounter bluebells, a clear indicator – as a woodland species – of the type of vegetation that used to exist. Bracken grows on nutrient-poor soil, but as the soil quality deteriorates it gives way to heath-type vegetation such as predominates on the Skiddaw Slates where the fellsides are bathed in the glorious purple of ling heather set against the dark green of bilberry.

Wherever the drainage is poor, bog-mosses occur along with cotton grass, especially on bare peat and around shallow pools. Most striking, however, is the vegetation of the cliffs, which varies according to altitude and geology. Around the low crags in Borrowdale, for example, where the rocks are acidic the outcrops are highly vegetated and colonised by bell heather, honeysuckle and ivy, and often have oak or rowan growing directly from fissures in the rocks. Where limestone occurs, you find yew and limestone trees and shrubs, such as whitebeam and privet, along with characteristic plants like vetch. On the screes below the crags, look for parsley fern which remarkably has managed to adapt to living on the very dry, well-drained screes.

Of course, a major feature of the Lake District are the streams, rivers and lakes, and each of these has a distinct vegetation which varies according to the type of rock the water has travelled through. Alongside mountains streams there is a variety of rushes, mosses and liverworts and, quite often, an Arctic-Alpine, starry saxifrage, but where the water has passed over calcite you find bird's-eye primrose and yellow saxifrage.

Mountain streams that flow into the steep-sided ravines, like Piers Gill and Dungeon Ghyll, have a humid atmosphere, and contain many of the same species as the mountain cliffs, notably mosses, liverworts and ferns. They also serve as a springboard for a surprising range of tree species which would spread out from the gills if the amount of grazing on the adjacent fellsides declined.

When the fall of the streams eases, so different conditions prevail, and here the streams are surrounded by meadowsweet, water celery, alder, ash and wych elm.

Where the streams and rivers meander as they approach the sea, common reed and reed canary grasses are well established.

An important factor determining the plants and animals found in the lakes is the level of nutrients. The two extremes are oligotrophic (nutrient poor) and eutrophic (nutrient rich). Lakes in between these two are mesotrophic. Most of the lakes in the Lake District are oligotrophic or mesotrophic. The main sources of nutrients are sewage, agriculture and fish farms. The more nutrient-rich lakes occur in the more intensively farmed and densely inhabited catchments, eg Windermere. The larger aquatic plants such as pondweeds and water lilies are best developed in mesotrophic waters. However, in the 1980s, it became clear that in some lakes the nutrient levels were increasing, threatening the aquatic plants and other species. Steps have been taken to reduce nutrient inputs, for example by phosphate stripping at sewage treatment works.

Visitors to Lakeland who enjoy naturalist exploration will find a life-long pursuit here. For these slower-moving folk the Lake District is a vast canvas of green dales, soaring fellsides, gullies and lakes on which are traced the location and movements of the region's wildlife.

There are few animals that make the mountain tops their home, the occasional bank vole, perhaps sustained by lunchtime crumbs from visiting walkers, but little else. There are, however, visiting birds such as snow bunting, which occasionally appear in winter, and dotterel, a delight to see, which are spring and autumn passage migrants. Also a pleasure is the mountain blackbird, the ring ouzel, but sadly their numbers have declined in recent years for as yet uncertain reasons.

Resident mute swans

Over the summits and among the crags that flank them, ravens reign supreme, usually identified first by their vocal 'crok' as they glide by overhead. They are stunning to watch, masters of the air, and surrounded by myths and tales of menace. Vying with them for cliff and air space are the Lake District's peregrines falcons. After a period of decline, largely due to the use of pesticides, peregrine have staged a recovery, and the National Park is now an important European breeding area for them.

The common buzzard, after a nationally bad spell when it was affected by pesticides and persecuted by gamekeepers, is now strong in the Lake District and progressing eastwards into the Vale of Eden and the north Pennines. This magnificent bird never fails to excite as it soars over the hills and dales, wheeling and turning in the air currents, and is often betrayed by its plaintive mewing cry, as evocative a sound of wild places as you could wish for.

But the most exciting event to hit the bird world of the Lake District was the return in the late 1960s, after an absence of over 200 years, of the golden eagle, now securely ensconced at the head of Haweswater, where they have bred (not always successfully) each year. They are the only golden eagles resident in England, and anyone wanting to see them should visit the manned public visitor point in Riggindale, which is open from April to the end of August.

The rolling fells above Haweswater are also the haunt of red deer, which have managed to adapt from their more traditional open woodland habitat to the harsh conditions on the fell tops. On a quiet day in autumn, you may well be privileged to hear one of the most evocative of Lakeland sounds; that of a red deer stag roaring at the rut.

The smaller roe deer, surely the most beautiful of our native animals, has steadily increased its range and population, and you may find them moving around in small family groups in early morning or at dusk, and it is not uncommon to find them in gardens, helping themselves to a change in diet. Road casualties of all ages occur, but unfortunately many kids are involved. Sadly, some are unwittingly doomed by people who find them concealed in bracken and, thinking them to be abandoned, try to pick them up. It is important not to do this: the doe conceals the kid deliberately, and returns at intervals to it to feed it. But once a kid carries human scent, its mother is unable to recognise it, and will abandon it.

The silence is also broken from time to time by a more startling sound, that of a female fox screaming for a mate. The fox is common on the fells, and is still hunted by the traditional Lakeland method – on foot.

Of especial delight to all visitors is the red squirrel population, which both enjoy the broadleaved woodlands and takes advantage of large gardens and bird tables. Unfortunately, elsewhere in England they struggle to survive against the invasive grey squirrels, which, cute as they may seem, ultimately oust them. This has not yet happened in the Lake District, though grey squirrels are now found along the Ambleside–Grasmere corridor and even as far north as Keswick.

Not all animals are quite so charming and inoffensive, though all are equally important to the ecosystem. Stoats and weasels are keen predators, and enjoy a young rabbit or two. You can often found these small, lithe bundles of red fur (the weasel is the smaller, while the stoat is the one with the black tip to its tail) concealed in dry-stone walls. In winter, the stoat turns ermine white, shedding its brown coat, but keeping the black tip to its tail. Dry-stone walls give shelter also to a small range of reptiles like common lizard, slow worm (actually a legless lizard, even though it looks like a snake), and adders. The adders are shy, and will usually slip away as humans approach, but occasionally they bask in the spring sunshine, warming up, and are quite often sluggish to move. They rarely bite, and their bite is not usually serious, but it is best avoided by having the good sense to observe any adders you see from a safe distance: only a fool would attempt to pick one up.

Less obvious to non-angling visitors are the inhabitants of the lakes and tarns. The nutrient-rich waters are populated by perch and pike, while sea trout, brown trout and salmon prefer the clearer, deeper water of rivers and lakes. One deepwater trout, the char, was a great Victorian delicacy, and Windermere potted char was much sought after. But two real relics survive from the last Ice Age: in Ullswater and Haweswater are shoals of schelly, a kind of freshwater herring, while Bassenthwaite and Derwent Water have populations of vendace, a rare whitefish, similar to the schelly.

Clearly, the great upheavals of geological times have contrived over millions of years to produce a vast range of habitats. To see and understand them all would take a lifetime.

Top: Roe deer grazing in the early morning
Above: An inquisitive stoat, seen near Caldbeck

3 Man's influence

Over the years, I've explored numerous nooks and crannies in Lakeland, but I especially remember a day during my time as a voluntary warden when I found myself wandering up Aaron Slack (between Great and Green Gable) and down the other side into Stony Cove in the upper reaches of Ennerdale.

It was an overcast day, the mist swirling across Windy Gap and occasionally parting to expose stunning cameos of Ennerdale. With me was one of the full-time wardens, bound for Buttermere on wardenly business.

Just below the mist, with sunlight slanting into the valley below, we perched among the rocks and had lunch. Being at the time largely unfamiliar with this part of Lakeland, I was receptive to everything, and mesmerised by the view and the eerily amplified sound of water tinkling through the rocks. It was a day for imagination, and even now, I need little encouragement to let mine run wild.

But for me, still very much a Lakeland novice, it was also to be a day of awakening because of the way a simple find led to a sudden realisation. Among the rocks at my feet, I saw a small sliver of rock that seemed different from those of which Great Gable was composed. It seemed too shapely to have been an accident, but it was my colleague who told me what it was, a fragment of a stone axe, made from tuff, the fine-grained compressed rocks of volcanic dust and ash produced during Ordovician times.

Prehistoric man, I knew, had an 'axe factory' on the slopes of the Langdale Pikes, and my find in upper Ennerdale could only mean that he may well have used the gap between the Gables as a direct route into Ennerdale and out to the coast. For me it was a sobering thought that someone from prehistoric times had not only walked past the very spot where I was having lunch, but may well have sat there himself, taking a breather after the climb up Aaron Slack.

Such possibilities are no doubt widespread throughout Lakeland and Britain, for the complex landscapes bear the imprint of man spanning six millennia. In the Lake District, this historical story has seven very distinct 'chapters'. Broadly speaking these seven elements cover the prehistoric period; the time of the Romans; the period of Anglo-Saxon

Left: Prehistoric Castlerigg stone circle, with Helvellyn beyond

Page 53: Earthworks near the stone circle on Kinniside Common

CAIRNS AND CIRCLES

Little is known about how Neolithic man lived. He would have constructed wooden buildings, but of these, nothing now remains. What does remain, however, are long cairns and stone circles that date from these distant times, late Neolithic and early Bronze Age. Sampson's Bratful on Stockdale Moor, north of Gosforth, is the only long cairn from this period that is accepted as such; others date from the Bronze Age.

Much has been written, and speculated, over the years about the purpose of stone circles, about their astronomical alignments, their geometric construction and their possible ritualistic function. But the truth is unknown, though it is a fair interpretation that they were of considerable ceremonial significance.

The best known of the stone circles is that at Castlerigg, east of Keswick, believed to date from about 3000BC. If this is correct, it pre-dates the great circles at Stonehenge and elsewhere. It is commonly regarded as the most superb stone circle of the many to be found in Cumbria, the most exciting and the most mysterious. It is certainly the most picturesque, set against a stunning backdrop of Lakeland fells. Enthusiasts of stone circles consider Castlerigg to be among the earliest stone circles in Europe. Poet John Keats, however, was not impressed, describing it as a 'dismal cirque, Of Druid stones, upon a forlorn moor' – though it certainly pre-dates the Druids by thousands of years.

Another attractive, but rather smaller, stone circle is that at Swinside, on the remote eastern edge of Black Combe, and there is another, damaged, circle at Elva Plain, east of Cockermouth.

and Norse colonisation; medieval times; the period of growing prosperity during the seventeenth and eighteenth centuries; the arrival of the railways and the large-scale development of mining and quarrying that took place during the nineteenth century, and finally the period of change witnessed during the twentieth century.

There is no certainty about when prehistoric man first arrived in the Lake District, and all that can be learned about him has to be gleaned from the few material items that have been found, and these begin with Mesolithic man (Middle Stone Age). He was primarily a hunter-gatherer who inhabited the coastal plains and the perimeter of the vast woodland that covered the region following the retreat of the last glaciers. Little remains of Mesolithic times, except harpoon barbs, arrow tips and a rudimentary settlement at Eskmeals on the Cumbrian coast, though a large find of Mesolithic flint tools was made at Drigg, north of Ravenglass.

The people who made the Langdale stone axes were Neolithic (New Stone Age), of a more recent era (roughly from the fourth to the early second millennium BC). Unlike their predecessors, they were farmers and grew crops, wore simple clothing, kept domestic animals and made crude pottery. The Langdale 'factory' was found in 1947, and axes from it were distributed throughout Britain in a very early form of trade, and many now reside in several of the country's museums.

But the prehistoric stone axe has even greater significance, for it was the implement used to make clearances in the forest and in so doing instigated an impact on the vegetation of the region from which it was never to recover. The stone axe was, in fact, the key that turned the once wooded landscape of Lakeland into the vastly denuded scene we see today, as Neolithic man made room in the forests for his domestic animals and for cultivation.

Remains of the early settlements in Lakeland are often difficult to identify or date precisely because later settlements have been superimposed upon them. Many burial mounds and cairns, often associated with settlements, were destroyed by amateur archaeologists during Victorian times, and sometimes what look like burial cairns are simply no more than piles of field clearance stones from some long disappeared system of agriculture.

Almost all of these burial sites are found around the perimeter of the Lake District, most on the coastal plain, including some sites used for burial by the Beaker people, thought to be of Iberian origin who spread out over Europe from the third millennium BC. They were capable metalworkers, but are more renowned for their use of distinctive earthenware beakers with various designs, of which the bell-beaker type was widely distributed throughout Europe. They favoured inhumation (burial of the intact body), often in round barrows, and secondary burials in some form of chamber tomb. A beaker accompanied each burial, possibly to hold a drink for the deceased on their final journey.

There are few archaeological features of the Iron Age presence in the Lake District. The characteristic hill-forts, enclosed by ditches and ramparts of earth or wood, are few in number here. The most distinguished is on the summit of Carrock Fell, north of Mungrisdale. It is very similar in many ways to the known hill-fort on Ingleborough in the Yorkshire Dales, but nothing has been discovered to date the Carrock Fell fort with any certainty. Today it is a bleak and windswept tumble of rocks, and authorities over the years have tried, unsuccessfully one feels, to blame the Romans for the destruction of the site, on the presumption that it was a Brigantian stronghold – the Brigantes were a loose coalition of Celtic tribes (in the Lake District the Carvettii) who ruled the greater part of northern England. It is just as likely that two millennia of Lakeland weather and the attentions of flocks

HARDKNOTT FORT

The most dramatic of all the Roman legacies must be the fort at Hardknott (Mediobogdum), perched on a windswept shelf above the Esk Valley, from which it could observe enemy activity. It held a formidable if bleak position, unlikely, one supposes, to be high on the list of favoured 'postings' – though it is a stunning place to be when the Lakeland weather is in a benevolent mood. From it the land fell away sharply on all sides save the north-east, where a defensive ditch was constructed. Hardknott Fort was built in the second century, during the reign of Hadrian (117–138), but it seems that it was not occupied continuously, and was largely abandoned by the end of the second century, and thereafter only used as a staging post.

Top: Ruins of the Roman bath house at Ravenglass   *Above: The Roman road across the upper slopes of High Street*

of sheep in the last few hundred years did the damage just as efficiently as the Romans might have.

Other hill-forts found within the National Park are at Castle Crag in Borrowdale, Castle Crag in Mardale and at Shoulthwaite Gill, north-west of Thirlmere.

The Roman military occupation of the Lake District overlaps with the native British Iron Age settlements. The Cumbrian people were well established by the time the Romans arrived. They were fishers and farmers, and both shrewd and strong enough ultimately to outlast the Roman presence. This began during the first century AD and continued until late in the fourth. Important features of their occupation remain evident today, some in the most dramatic of settings. Throughout the early part of this period, the Romans fought a constant, running battle against the Brigantes, who took every advantage of the convoluted topography in which each fold in the fells was a potential ambush site or place of concealment from which to launch guerrilla raids.

The Romans probably first reached the edge of the Lake District from York, where they already had a base, but it seems to have been from Chester that the main 'invasion' was launched, under the command of Gnaeus Julius Agricola, in AD79. His approach was to build roads and defend them at intervals with forts. The main thrust of their road system ran northwards, touching upon the Lakeland fringe at Watercrook, east of Kendal, and then continuing via Brougham to Penrith and Carlisle. Within the National Park there are only a few roads and auxiliary forts.

From Watercrook one road ran north-westwards towards Ambleside, where the Romans built their fort at Borrans Field (*Galava*) at Waterhead. From it, a road probably ran through Troutbeck to the high ground of the eastern fells. The Roman road across High Street, which may well have followed the line of an existing prehistoric route to avoid poor conditions in the valleys, continued to the fort at Brougham (*Brocavum*).

The first construction at Borrans Field would have been of timber and turf, and later rebuilt in stone. From it an uncommonly indirect road was constructed through the tortured terrain of Little Langdale and Duddon, via the Wrynose Pass and Hardknott to Eskdale and Ravenglass, where a supply port was built (*Glannaventa*). The bath house here, known as Walls Castle, still stands to a considerable height, though much of the fort was damaged by the railway.

There is a tendency to picture the Roman occupation as a particularly turbulent period, one of domination and oppression. In reality, it produced a prolonged period of peace and prosperity that blossomed not only from the supervision and encouragement that the Roman presence afforded, but from the trade routes that their roads opened up. In a number of places, the farmsteads of the native population survive in the dales of Lakeland, notably in Bannisdale, Glencoyne Park and Grisedale to the west of Ullswater, though they are less well known than farmsteads further east and outside the National Park boundary.

For how long these farm holdings continued to be occupied after the Romans had left is not certain. Increasingly, as the Romans started to leave Britain, the local people began to rely on their own resources. They may have built new settlements, moving further away from the Roman sites as building materials became exhausted or the need for improved self-sufficiency sent them in search of better land to farm and places easier to defence against rival factions among the tribes that remained.

But in the Lake District and wider Cumbria, it is especially difficult to tell with certainty how the county evolved between the fifth and twelfth centuries, and there are many conflicting accounts.

CROSSES AND TOMBSTONES

The finest surviving monuments of Anglian and Viking times are the stone crosses and hogback tombstones. Most of these are outside the National Park, but there are fine crosses at Irton and Waberthwaite. At Dacre, four weathered sculptures of bears are of uncertain origin, but the church houses fragments of two Anglo-Saxon crosses. This site also seems to have been the location of a pre-Conquest monastery where archaeological research has exposed part of a cemetery, a wooden building, drainage channels and other Anglo-Saxon artefacts.

On the other side of the Lake District, at Gosforth, is a Viking wheel-headed cross (pictured below), probably early eleventh century, carved in sandstone and depicting scenes that fuse Norse mythology and Christian events. The church at Gosforth contains two hogback tombstones and other stone fragments.

The River Kent at Kendal

Pages 58–9: Norse influence:
Rosthwaite and Stonethwaite in
Borrowdale from Castle Crag

During the fifth century, Cumbria grew into a British kingdom called Rheged, one that probably encompassed land on both sides of the Solway. By the end of the sixth century, Rheged, for a time a major political force in the north, had faded from the scene, and what remained of it was enveloped by the expanding kingdom of Northumbria, possibly by marriage rather than conquest.

By the early tenth century, however, the Anglian kingdom of Northumbria fell before the onslaught of the Vikings, leaving a vacuum that was filled by the kingdom of Strathclyde. In 945, King Edmund of Northumbria defeated the king of Strathclyde, Malcolm I, but ceded all of Cumbria to Malcolm, provided that Malcolm should be his 'helper on land and sea'. In spite of this, Cumbria, which is a difficult commodity to identify with certainty today, seems to have continued under its own line of kings until 1018. In that year, the last Cumbrian king, Owen the Bald, allied himself with Malcolm II of Scotland, and was later killed in battle against the English. Consequently, Malcolm was free to annex Cumbria into Scotland, and so it remained until 1032, when King Cnut (Canute) exchanged Lothian for Cumbria.

During this period came the settlement of the Scandinavians, mainly Norse. It was their influence that gave the Lake District many of its place-names: tarn is derived from *tjorn*, dale from *dahl*, and fell from *fjall*. While the suffix '-thwaite', which means a clearing, crops up in many places – Stonethwaite, Rosthwaite, Bassenthwaite, Braithwaite, and so on.

Nothing is mentioned in the Domesday Book about the county we know as Cumbria, for by 1068 all the lands north of the Derwent and the Eamont had been seized by Malcolm III, and the boundary of Scotland once more embraced much of Lakeland. But by the end of the eleventh century, Norman barons were heading north in search of wealth, some of them as colonists brought north by William Rufus, who in 1092 had redeemed the balance of power in England's favour when he marched north with a large army and built a castle at Carlisle.

The influence of the Norman barons on the landscape was considerable. They had a strong liking for hunting, and developed many of the hunting forests that once covered the region, and whose names you still find across the modern map – Skiddaw, Inglewood and Copeland. But their most important legacy was the monasteries, though most are outside the present National Park boundary. During the twelfth century, monasteries were founded at Wetheral (1106), St Bees (1120), Furness (1123), Holme Cultram (1150) and Shap (1200). In turn, the monasteries became immense landowners, spreading well into the mountain areas and cultivating ground that had previously remained barren. Kendal Castle, now a ruin, also dates from this time, to which additional features were added during the thirteenth and fourteenth centuries. It was the home of the barons of Kendal and their centre of administration and defence. Catherine Parr (1512–48), the last wife of Henry VIII, was born in the castle, at which time it was owned by her father, Sir Thomas Parr; by the end of the century it was in an advanced state of decay.

With the development of the monasteries, however, came much-improved documentary records that give a clearer picture of life in the Lake District from then on.

Farms, and the cottages and hamlets that evolved around them were instrumental in determining the settlement pattern of Cumbria, and the key to this lies in the system of feudalism that existed. The pattern evolved around great baronial estates, and though much of the land was designated as 'forest' or 'chase' – in both cases meaning a place for hunting – the lords of the estates tolerated the development of peasant communities, and so created embryonic villages.

Top: Barn roof detail, Hartsop
Above: Water wheel, Stock Ghyll, Ambleside

Left: Dixon Ground farm, Coniston

LAKELAND STATESMEN

The evolution of statesmen farmers is fascinating. What we now know as Cumbria was then Cumberland, Westmorland and Lancashire-North-of-the-Sands. The region was never organised on a manorial basis in quite the same way, nor to the same extent, as counties further south, and though serfdom was not unknown, it seems probable that the proportion of tenants who were 'free' was much higher. A large though indeterminate part of the population in Elizabethan times held their land by a tenure of obscure origin known as tenant-right. This varied from place to place in its detail, but in Borrowdale, for example, included a custom that tenants should be ready to serve in battle against the Scots. Provided this custom was observed (and, of course, the rent duly paid), their land was secure to them and their heirs. The Union of the Crowns in 1603 ostensibly ended the needed for 'Border' service, and so James I tried to abolish tenant-right. That he failed is a tribute to the tenacity of some remarkable and courageous statesmen of the time. During the sixteenth century, landlords became even more dissatisfied with fixed rents and tried to exact fines on change of tenancy, or endeavoured to get the yeomen farmers to accept leases in place of the 'estates of inheritance', as they were called. There was limited success in this, but the statesmen survived into the eighteenth century, extending their holdings and buying freedom from service and succession payments. By the time Wordsworth wrote about them, the number of statesman farmers had greatly declined, and continued to do so.

In the centuries that followed there was a period of sustained population growth, and almost every county in England had farms and small hamlets carved from the rugged and wild landscapes that surrounded the baronial estates.

By 1300, the Lakeland dales were widely populated, but the state of evolving peace was to be shattered by the waves of destruction that flowed during the time of the Border Troubles, and by the incidence of the Black Death (1348–9). For 150 years, the development of Lakeland villages was held in check: what was built, was knocked down; what was grown, was stolen. This state of affairs lasted until the Union of the Crowns in 1603 (and beyond), but much earlier than that a tide of change swept across Cumbria and the Lake District with the growth of the woollen cloth industry, notably in Kendal. Once again population levels increased, and provoked a demand for land which soon could only be satisfied by expanding beyond existing holdings.

Wealth came not only from farming produce, but also from taking surplus or short-lived goods to markets held in the ancient market towns of Cumbria, though there are only a few within the National Park boundary. Ambleside received its market charter in 1650, and Bootle originally in the fourteenth century, during the reign of Edward III, a concession that was renewed by Elizabeth I in 1567. The importance of market charters was considerable and even today Broughton-in-Furness celebrates its charter, which is read out at the Market Cross on the first day of August each year. Kendal, just outside the National Park boundary, was granted a market charter in 1189 by Richard I, and since 1989 has celebrated the fact in an annual Medieval Market, held in May.

The period between 1550 and 1700 saw 'statesmen' farmers flourishing. This term, romanticised by Wordsworth, was applied to small, family farmers whose tenure in effect gave them security equivalent to freehold. It was by their efforts that the dales of the Lake District and beyond were carved into small 'estates'; and these in turn were a key factor in shaping the human landscape.

But the presence of these 'independent' farmers did much to develop the land-scape of the Lake District. Wherever there was an area of viable ploughland or hay

meadow in the valley bottom, so a communal form of farming evolved. These
'townfields' were areas of arable land and meadow serving a group of farms, and
so forming a small village or hamlet. Examples of this are to be found at Coniston,
Grasmere, Buttermere, and Braithwaite near Keswick where towards the end of
the sixteenth century there was a small village of sixteen farmsteads in an open
landscape. Elsewhere, lesser groups of farms developed into the small hamlets that
still exist today. But whether large or small, the pattern was much the same: each
farmstead held a small patch of ploughland and meadow, along with common
rights over the fellside pastures that flanked the dales.

But this was not a constant process. During the next 150 years, many Lakeland
communities decreased in size as farms were amalgamated into fewer, larger holdings. Much of this was done piecemeal as farmers agreed to consolidate their
holdings, often on an informal and unrecorded basis. But the result was a gradual
drawing together of communities; some expanded, others contracted.

And in the same way that settlements evolved around the viable agricultural
land, so they sprang up, in some cases almost overnight, once the exploitation of
Cumbria's mineral wealth took off. What was Coniston without its copper, or
Whitehaven without its coal and the means to export it seaward, or Shap without
its granite, or Borrowdale without the lead for the pencil industry that developed
in Keswick? Across the whole face of the Lake District, communities evolved to
serve the needs of industry – copper, lead, graphite, tungsten, iron ore, coal, stone
and limestone. In some cases further industries developed to serve or benefit from
the earlier ones – iron smelting bloomeries needed charcoal, as did the charcoal-
fuelled blast furnaces; mills of all kinds took advantage of the abundant water
supply to power the production of bobbins, gunpowder, textiles and paper.

*Above: Reconstruction of a charcoal
burner's hut, Grizedale Forest*

*Opposite: Slater's Bridge, Little
Langdale*

All that remained was to link all these places together. Reliance on Roman roads, packhorse routes, monastic ways and the traditional mountain passes was no longer good enough. The network of roads that evolved in the eighteenth and nineteenth centuries was instrumental in securing the economic, social and political development of the county. With the coming of the turnpikes, the die was cast. It was only in 1761 that the first turnpike within the modern National Park boundary appeared. This ran from Kendal through Ambleside, via Dunmail Raise to Keswick and Cockermouth.

One brief period, however, during the nineteenth century, is worthy of special mention, for between 1850 and 1860 the development of the Lake District crossed an important watershed. During this short time, the pace of change in the Lake District quickened noticeably, in good measure inspired by the coming of the railway. Bringing a new breed of tourist, who proved to be a catalyst to the changes already under way, the railway was an important factor. It reached Windermere first, in 1847, Coniston in 1859 and Keswick in 1864. Wordsworth was very much against the railway reaching much further into the heart of Lakeland, as the railway moguls wanted, and took the view that the tranquillity of Lakeland would be disrupted by hordes of day-trippers from the not-so-distant Lancashire cotton towns. John Ruskin also spoke out against the railways, which he felt would bring about ''the deterioration of the moral character in the inhabitants'. Harriet Martineau, however, took an opposing view, saying that 'the residents may find that their minds will have become more stirred and enlarged by intercourse with strangers who have, from circumstance, more vivacity and faculty and a wider knowledge'.

But it wasn't only the cause of tourism that was served by the railways. In 1857, the Coniston Railway Company was formed principally to transport copper from the mines above Coniston. The line opened in 1859 and ran through Torver to Broughton-in-Furness, where it connected with the Furness Railway. The copper mines at Coniston flourished between 1854 and 1875, and while they did so, the railway was a viable concern. After mining had almost ended, towards the end of the nineteenth century, the line had to rely solely on tourism, and was less successful in doing so than its counterpart serving Windermere.

Another mine-serving line, one that remains to this day, but not in its original form, runs through the lower reaches of Eskdale. It was built in 1875 to transport iron ore from the mines at Boot, but also carried tourists. This line, too, suffered badly when the mines closed, but is currently enjoying a massive revival as the Ravenglass and Eskdale Railway.

In the north of the Lake District, a single line connected with existing railways at Penrith and Cockermouth, via Keswick. It is still in use today, but now only to serve walkers and cyclists.

Tourism, however, is the key to the greatest incidence of social and economic change in the Lake District in the nineteenth and twentieth centuries. As the number of tourists grew, so did the 'industries' necessary to meet their needs, and an increasing number of innkeepers, shopkeepers, servants and tradespeople focused on centres like Bowness, Windermere and Keswick. The old industries – textile production, charcoal-burning, gunpowder manufacture, mining and quarrying, the latter once having employed up to 7,000 men – have almost entirely gone. Of the old times, only the sheep remain, and even now their farmers are having a difficult time.

Top: The wreckage of a World War II Halifax bomber on the summit of Great Carrs
Above: The Ravenglass and Eskdale Railway at Dalegarth station

Opposite: Red Dell Works, Coppermines Valley, Coniston

4 Land use, culture and customs

Below: Field pattern near Stool End, Great Langdale

Opposite: Troutbeck Park and Ill Bell, showing the transition from intake fields to rough fell pasture

The Lake District National Park is a special place; a fact recognised nationally and internationally. It is a vital area of intrinsic landscape beauty, combining spectacular and craggy fells and delectable dales, tarns and lakes. It has been and remains a source of inspiration for writers, painters and naturalists, but above all it continues to provide enjoyment to millions of people, who derive pleasure from the wild and beautiful countryside, in many parts remote, peaceful and quiet.

But the Lake District is also a place where people live and work, where the land is used in a multiplicity of ways. It is, too, a region with an identifiable culture of its own, its own traditions, its own customs and folklore, and its own heritage.

Farming may not be instantly appreciated as a vital component of that heritage, although farming has been present, in one form or another, since prehistoric times. It has shaped much of the character and appearance of today's landscape, which is very much a product of traditional farming practices followed by generations of Lakeland farmers. Features such as the field patterns, the simple vernacular farm buildings, field barns, dry-stone walls, hedgerows, trees, woodlands and copses do much to enrich the landscape and are all testimony to the key importance of farming.

Compared to the large arable farms of southern England, Lakeland farming must seem small and old fashioned, but it is the product of many an individual family's labour, for some of the Lakeland farms have been continued by the same family for generations. It is this continuity that has enabled most of the farms to survive – though family farms are diminishing in number – but another key factor has been the policy of the National Trust in acquiring and preserving traditional Lakeland farms. Currently, the Trust owns ninety-three farms and in excess of 25,000 Herdwick sheep. Beatrix Potter, who gifted a number of farms to the Trust, wanted the breed preserved, and so they are, for they do well on the Lakeland fells. You will also find some crossbreeds, produced by bringing Herdwicks and Swaledales together, and many farmers prefer these.

Woodlands and plantations, which occupy approximately 67,000 acres (27,000ha), are another important land use feature of the Lake District. They contribute significantly to the diversity of the landscape and, since a complete reversal in the 1960s of the Forestry Commission policy that precluded public access to their holdings, provide wonderful opportunities for quiet public enjoyment. They include two National Forest Parks, at Grizedale and Whinlatter, while the predominantly broadleaved semi-natural woodlands are recognised as among the Lake District's most valuable scenic and wildlife assets. A large proportion of the broadleaved woods are recorded as ancient semi-natural woodland sites.

The Lake District has a diverse geology and is rich in mineral deposits. Especially important is slate quarrying, which began originally as underground workings centuries ago, but has continued more recently as surface workings. There are now fewer, but larger, slate quarries within the National Park. Underground mining for minerals, notably lead, copper, graphite and tungsten reached a peak during Victorian times, and the past influence of the industry has had a major impact on the character and appearance of the Park and on its landscape.

Mineral production is now limited and concentrates on slate, stone and aggregates. There are three large-scale quarries, at Elterwater, Broughton Moor and Kirkstone, and others see more periodic activity as the demand for a particular slate, for example, arises. There are two granite quarries just outside the National Park boundary at Shap and two limestone quarries that straddle the boundary at Kendal Fell and Shap. The industry employs over 200 people, and remains a significant employer in places like Langdale and Coniston.

Water, of course, is an ever-present feature of the Lakeland landscape. There are about twenty principal lakes and hundreds of tarns of varying shapes and sizes. Some of the lakes are used for recreation, but others supply drinking water to distant conurbations.

Many visitors to the Lake District, from those conurbations, for example, are short-stay outsiders coming in for recreation and enjoyment. But before the influx of tourists, what did those who already lived here, in what was still a remote and rather wild area, do to amuse themselves?

Well, the oldest of the traditional sports of fell country are fox hunting and wrestling. Chasing foxes, of course, was part of the daily way of life, and done to protect sheep rather than for any sporting pleasure it might have brought. It is just another job, like rebuilding dry-stone walls, and, unlike lowland hunting, is done on foot, requiring a good heart and lungs for all involved.

A few years ago, I perched among the rocks of Striding Edge and watched the hunt range at alarming speed over St Sunday Crag opposite, seldom on the easiest line of ascent, only to plunge down into Grisedale and race past me, crossing

THE FARMER'S YEAR

For many people, a trip to the Lake District can be timed to coincide with a favourable slot in the weather, but for the Lakeland farmer the weather is an occupational hazard or a blessing, according to what it's doing and which tasks need to be carried out. Lakeland farming follows an age-old plan that has changed little over the years. Although the early months of the year do bring new-born lambs to the dale pastures, most lambs are born from April onwards. By the end of May, they are moved onto the fells with the ewes. Haymaking usually begins in June, but depends very much on the weather. July and August see the farmer busy with the sheep, dipping and clipping before the lamb sales in September and ewe sales in October. Throughout the winter months the hard work continues, for then it is that the farmer must ensure that the flocks out on the fells are fed and don't become trapped by blizzards. Once the rams, or 'tups', are among the ewes, so the cycle begins again.

Opposite: (top) Annual sheep gathering, at Seathwaite, Borrowdale; (below) the shepherd's year moves on into winter above Great Langdale

Overleaf: Thirlmere, one of Lakeland's reservoirs, from the slopes of Helvellyn. A low water level has exposed the shoreline

below Red Tarn before climbing across the bottom of Swirral Edge and disappearing from sight, all, it seemed, in a matter of minutes. On this occasion, I was sure the fox was safely 'earthed' deep among the rocks only fifty yards from where I sat, because I'd seen him go in there. I could only presume the hounds had picked up a different scent.

Wrestling in the Cumberland and Westmorland style may flummox the casual observer, for it seems to comprise little more than two men hugging one another prior to falling down in a heap. That, of course, does the sport a disservice for it is highly technical and involves attempting to lure your opponent into a position of seeming security before quickly getting him off balance and throwing him down. The rules are quite simple: the two opponents stand with arms locked behind each other's back and the winner is the one who succeeds in throwing his opponent to the ground. If they both fall, the man on top is adjudged the winner. Nor is mere strength the secret, though many of the winners do appear sturdy and well built.

A sport involving hounds, as distinct from the occupation of fox hunting, is that of hound trailing. Trail hounds, as they are known, are bred and trained for an altogether different purpose than hunting hounds.

Hound trailing is fascinating to watch, but best observed from high on the fellsides across the valley from where the trail has been set. Binoculars are an indispensable aid. The whole sport is highly organised, and has a ruling body founded in 1906.

The trail is 'laid' by men dragging old stockings or suchlike, filled with an official mixture strongly flavoured with aniseed, across the fells. This is the route the hounds will follow, and, as they do so, it is difficult not to become engrossed in the excitement. For much of the time the hounds will be out of sight – one of the reasons why a high vantage point helps – but as soon as they re-appear a buzz ripples through the spectators, and the catchers begin a fantastic and energetic finale of whistles, calls, pleas and curses that would do a Strauss symphony proud. The leaders leap the last few walls with apparent ease before dashing down the field to their handlers and a waiting bowl of food.

In similar vein, but this time with humans coursing the fells, is the fairly localised but popular sport of fell running. With some direct experience, I can speak of its breath-taking exhilaration and physical demands. There can surely be no fitness greater than that required to run for miles over high mountains or up and down the nearest steep fellside, and no excitement to surpass that of careering full tilt down a long grassy fellside. For many runners, it is as much a competition with oneself as against fellow athletes.

The sport of fell running began a long time ago, no one seems to recall when exactly, but there was a 'Guides' Race' at Grasmere in 1852, the first occasion for which records still remain. These races remain one of the main attractions to the dales sports, and though it has spread further afield, it was born in Lakeland fell country.

Also conceived in the fell country of Cumbria and the Lake District is a catalogue of myths, legends and folklore, most having their roots in the Dark Ages, when superstition was rife and tales of the supernatural a feature of everyday life. Many, indeed most, of the ancient traditions have long since died out, though rush-bearing, for example, is still observed in a few villages. Elsewhere, all that remains is a fine legacy of wonderful stories of nature lore (a cock crowing near the door meant a stranger would soon arrive), calendar lore (by Candlemas Day – 2 February – all geese should lay), the Lucks of Cumbria (such as the Luck of Edenhall – a Syrian

THE LAKE POETS

The foundation of a Lakeland tradition was laid when, in the eighteenth century, 'Romantic' interest in the area first developed. And it was the so-called 'Lake Poets' that we must credit with changing the way people felt about the Lake District and saw into the life of things. Among these, William Wordsworth was foremost, but, perhaps sadly, few can recall any of his works other than one that concerns daffodils. Yet he was almost singularly instrumental in attracting fellow poets to the Lakes.

From Wordsworth's vast outpouring, it is perhaps in his Guide to the Lakes *that we see more balanced and perceptive observation, a blend of romantic jargon and careful attention to detail that has given valuable insight into the Lakeland of his day. Nor should we ignore the writings of his sister, Dorothy, for although not a poet in the accepted sense, nevertheless had many poetic things to say and, more to the point, kept detailed records of daily life ('I sate mending stockings all the morning') combined with passages of some observational intensity ('The sky to the north was of a chastened yet rich yellow fading into pale blue and streaked and scattered over with steady islands of purple melting away into shades of pink. It made my heart almost feel like a vision to me').*

Opposite: The Junior Fell Race at Eskdale Show

Rydal Mount, Wordsworth's home.
The dining room is part of the
original cottage

glass goblet, now in the Victoria and Albert Museum), and legend (of kings, of wizards, and of spectral armies).

With so much fascinating raw material to work with it is hardly surprising that those visitors gifted with words did much to describe and perpetuate the essence of the Lake District, and that so many unique and flamboyant characters emerged as a result. Such eminent names as those of Wordsworth, Coleridge, Southey, de Quincey, Harriet Martineau and Beatrix Potter spring instantly to mind. The places where they were born, educated or lived in later life, and the landscape they gazed out on each day, hold great charisma for visitors, and have been fully documented in numerous publications.

But there are others, some much less well known, who made their contributions to the literature of the Lake District, too. Celia Fiennes, Daniel Defoe, Thomas Pennant and Joshua Budworth were outsiders looking in, as distinct from those who lived here, though their accounts are no less valid for that. But how far back do you go in making literary associations? Does the twelfth century count, when a monk at Furness Abbey wrote about St Mungo, better known in Lakeland as St Kentigern? He was made Bishop of Cumbria in AD543, and has seven churches named after him in the county of Cumbria, plus two as St Mungo. More recently, Richard Braithwaite of Burneside wrote in 1635 about a ferry disaster on Windermere in which forty-seven people were drowned. He and other minor but gifted poets now almost forgotten – Thomas Tickell of Bridekirk and Thomas Hoggart of Troutbeck – wrote poignant verses, often found carved on gravestones.

In a sense, it is academic; there have been so many wonderful things written about the Lake District that a shelf that contains them all is one that groans under the weight.

Beyond the coterie of the Lake Poets, there were few literary talents who at some stage did not visit the Lake District, though not all are, even now, household names. Liverpool-born poet Felicia Hemans lived at Dove Nest overlooking Windermere. She is remembered for her poem *Casabianca*, better known as 'The boy stood on the burning deck'. It was in the Lakes that Charlotte Brontë first met her biographer-to-be, Elizabeth Gaskell; Charles Dickens and novelist Wilkie Collins climbed to the remote, craggy summit of Carrock Fell, and Tennyson often stayed at Mire House overlooking Bassenthwaite Lake, where he wrote *Idylls of the King*. Tennyson also spent his honeymoon in the Lake District, staying at Tent Lodge, near Coniston, where his photograph was taken by Lewis Carroll.

There are, of course, other writers with a great passion for the Lake District, many of whom came to live in the area. Harriet Martineau, born in Norwich, came to live in Ambleside in 1845. In 1871, John Ruskin bought Brantwood above Coniston, apparently without even seeing the house, working on the belief that any location looking across a the Old Man of Coniston *must* be beautiful. What he found necessitated much work before it became the fine mansion it remains to this day, and it was his home for almost the last thirty years of his life.

Canon Rawnsley, one of the founders of the National Trust, wrote prolifically about the Lake District towards the end of the nineteenth century, while from the twentieth century come the works of Sir Hugh Walpole, whose *Herries Chronicles* did much to encourage readers to explore Lakeland. More recent authors of note are Melvyn Bragg, born in Wigton, who wrote novels that portray a deep understanding of the Cumbrian personality and landscapes, notably *For Want of a Nail*, *The Hired Man* and *The Maid of Buttermere*. Molly Lefebure, Harry Griffin and Lancashire-born Jessica Lofthouse have all written about Lakeland with great insight, depth and feeling. John Wyatt, former chief warden of the National Park, expressed his affection for Lakeland in his two evocatively written books *Shining Levels* and *Reflections on the Lakes*.

But perhaps the greatest Lakeland poet of modern times is Norman Nicholson, who lived at Millom, just outside the National Park, all his life. He received the Queen's Gold Medal for Poetry and the OBE. Sadly, he died in 1987. As well as producing volumes of verse, Nicholson also wrote topographical books like *Portrait of the Lakes*, the classic *The Lakers*, and *Greater Lakeland*.

Nor was it only poets or topographical writers who produced works about the Lake District, children's authors, too, have been prolific in using Lakeland settings for their books. Arthur Ransome's *Swallows and Amazons*, Rosemary Sutcliff's *The Shield Ring*, and Marjorie Lloyd's *Fell Farm Holiday*. And, of course, Beatrix Potter, many of whose books about animal fantasies were written while living at Hill Top at Near Sawrey.

It is probably unknown how many books have been written about the Lake District; more than 50,000 according to one estimate, and the total grows at an alarming rate. But that in itself speaks volumes; if so much could be written, there must be so much to write about – so much history and beauty, so much variety and fascination, so much hope and frustration, but, above all else, so much satisfaction.

The grave of Arthur Ransome and his wife Evgenia in Rusland churchyard

5 Recreation

Initially, it was the waterfalls and viewing the 'set' landscapes that were the main reasons for people to come to the Lakes, but gradually guidebooks devoted more space to the surrounding summits as mountain walking and then rock climbing became more popular.

The earliest records of visitors walking on the mountains date from the end of the eighteenth century, but interest became intensified during the early part of the nineteenth. Thomas West, in *A Guide to the Lakes* (first published in 1778 and which by 1821 had gone through a further nine editions) commented: 'Since persons of genius, taste and observation began to make the tour of their own country – the spirit has diffused itself among the curious of all ranks.' What should not be overlooked, however, in a quest for 'firstness', is the fact that long before tourists appeared the local shepherds will certainly have wandered extensively over the fells caring for their flocks. And long before them, prehistoric man will have crossed the tops, or at least some of them, in pursuit of his next meal.

In 1823, Jonathan Otley, a Keswick guide later looked upon by many as the father of Lakeland geology, produced the wonderfully titled book, *A Concise Description of the English Lakes, The Mountains in their vicinity, And the Roads by which they may be visited; With Essays on Mineralogy and Geology, on Meteorology, the Floating Island on*

Opposite: Ken Forsythe on Gimmer Crag; a popular rock-climbing venue. Great Langdale and Wetherlam visible

Page 78: Napes Needle, Great Gable, first climbed by Haskett Smith in 1886

Below: The old track to Gatescarth Pass, Longsleddale, a remote Lakeland valley

Derwent Lake, and the Black-Lead Mine in Borrowdale, and Map of the District.
Unlike other books of the time, which were purely descriptive of the landscape,
Otley's was the first 'directing the tourist through the most eligible paths'.

The guidebook coincided with a steadily growing tide of visitors. This was
an era when the romantic was seen in terms of nature's grandeur, and, paradoxically (given the persistence with which they were to come), 'horror' and
mountains were inextricably linked. Many of the early pioneers to 'the Lake
Mountains' were seen as cranks, but among them were some who saw the
mountains as a source of enjoyment and places that afforded magnificent views.
Hutchinson, the Cumberland historian, for example, climbed Skiddaw in the
early 1770s, and observed 'The prospect which we gained from the eminence
very well rewarded the fatigue'. For John Ruskin, who spent the last years of his
life at Brantwood above Coniston Water, mountains were 'the beginning and
the end of all natural scenery'.

During the nineteenth century, walking was a serious and involved affair,
and climbing a Lake District mountain approached in much the same way as
an Alpine summit. Ponies were used to transport equipment and refreshments,
and guides were hired. But gradually, 'mountains' became 'fells', and soon it
was commonplace to find many of the valleys echoing to the sound of walkers
as the pursuit of fell walking took on a new pace.

To begin with, it was groups of students from the universities, notably
Oxford and Cambridge, who gathered at the dale heads to explore the mountains. Wasdale Head in particular became something of a Mecca, and it was
not unusual to find the hotel there fully booked. From this base, walkers and
climbers would range into the fine ring of summits from Yewbarrow, around
the head of Mosedale, over Pillar onto Kirk Fell and Great Gable, and by Sty
Head to Great End, the Scafells and Lingmell. It remains something of a
romantic idea that you can wander all day across the fell tops and descend,
weary but happy, into some distant valley and find a bed for the night. The
reality, especially in spring and summer, is likely to be disappointment, unless
you are carrying your bed and shelter on your back.

Other dales, too, proved popular, as they still are – Langdale, Eskdale and
Borrowdale – and here walkers and climbers happily disappear for a few hours
into their own worlds among the rocks and gullies. It is in exploring freely that
you can most appreciate what a wonderful resource the Lake District is.
Although the fells are, compared say with the Alps, upwardly challenged, they
are nevertheless a test for everyone, even the most experienced, and should not
be dismissed because so few of them exceed a modest 3,000ft (and none exceeds
1,000m); to do so is to raise mere altitude to an elevation it does not deserve.

In the early days, fell walking was both a way of enjoyment for the individual and something to be experienced as part of a group of ramblers. A number
of organisations developed to offer fell walking holidays, notably the Co-oper-
ative Holidays Association and the Holiday Fellowship. These provided a way
for many newcomers to fell walking to learn the basic skills, even if it meant
plodding along behind a leader at the pace of the slowest member. From these
organised beginnings many walkers have gone on to find their own inspiration
among the fells.

As the numbers of walkers grew, so the problem of access first reared its
head elsewhere in Britain, and between the First and Second World Wars
pressure to address the question of freedom to wander over the hills gathered

THE WAINWRIGHT LEGACY

*In no small way, the development of fell
walking during the second half of the
twentieth century, can be attributed to the
work of Alfred Wainwright, sometime Borough
Treasurer of Kendal, who, over a period of
thirteen years, produced his classic collection
of Pictorial Guides to the Lakeland Fells. The
first, after a couple of years gestation,
appeared in 1955, and the last in 1966.
They were never revised and, consequently,
being between thirty and forty-plus years old,
are now inaccurate in some detail if not in
general. But they are unquestionably unique
and amazingly skilful works of art, although
as practical guides they have been replaced
by a vast and largely well-written selection of
up-to-date books by contemporary authors.*

*Today, enjoyment of the Lakeland fells
and dales is aided by the fact that the Lake
District has one of the heaviest
concentrations of youth hostels and outdoor
pursuit centres in the country. They have an
important role to play in providing access to
the countryside for many people at quite
low cost.*

*Of course, there is a downside to the
area's popularity with walkers. Many parts
of the Lakeland District are groaning under
the pressure of thousands of booted feet,
and erosion is a major problem that both
the National Park and the National Trust
have had to address with some urgency. The
worst spots include the ascent of Helm
Crag, the ridge of Cat Bells, and the way up
onto Scafell Pike from Wasdale. But you can
see the evidence of erosion almost
anywhere. It is easily started: the soil does
not support luxurious vegetation, and is
subjected to widely variable temperature
and weather conditions. Boots create grooves
that expand into rainwater channels, and
the result is wash-out. The path becomes
muddy and unpleasant to walk, so walkers
move further away from the worst line, and
in so doing simply expand the problem.
There is no easy or cheap solution, but the
problem has been countered in some places
by the construction of pitched pathways,
made of stone.*

STEP BY STEP

Since the days of the Abraham brothers, the number of climbing routes in the Lake District has reached monumental proportions, and cater for all standards of climber. It is interesting to note, however, that George Abraham in Complete Mountaineer, *published in 1907, wrote 'Nowadays it is extremely difficult to find a new feasible route on any of the bigger crags… It is no exaggeration to say that some of the British climbs have reached the border line where the law of gravity exerts itself and human muscles and endurance cannot prevail.' But the history of rock climbing is hallmarked by a series of 'steps' beyond which, for a time, progress seemed impossible. Then a new step would be taken, by a new climber on the scene, and a new standard achieved. This process apparently seems to continue.*

Opposite: (top) Looking over Ennerdale from Steeple; one of Lakeland's finest rounds; (below) the circuit of Derwent Water is a popular walk

momentum. In the Lake District, however, access has rarely been a major issue, because of the massive network of rights of way, great tolerance by landowners of access over the fells, and by the fact that the National Trust owns so much land to which walkers seek access.

Returning to the history of Lakeland recreation, it was only a matter of time before pedestrian exploration of the fells was extended into a closer affinity with the rocks themselves. In 1881, Walter Parry Haskett Smith came to the Lake District with fellow students from Oxford to walk on the fells. The next year he returned and began climbing the rocks for their own sake, a pursuit into which he persuaded his brother. It was this notion of climbing rocks for themselves that has posted Haskett Smith into posterity as the founder of British rock climbing. It was in 1886 that he made his most famous climb: the first ascent of Napes Needle on Great Gable, which he climbed solo. Later he climbed with another great pioneer, John Wilson Robinson, who climbed Pillar Rock in 1882, and made over a hundred ascents of the crag. Robinson was not the first to tackle Pillar Rock, however; this is credited to John Atkinson who climbed the Rock in 1826, an event recorded in the local press at the time. More than twenty years earlier, Coleridge descended from Scafell to Mickledore by the route now known as Broad Stand, and penned an accurate description of his experience in the journal of his tour of the Lake District in that year.

In 1894, Haskett Smith published *Climbing in the British Isles, England*, the first rock climbing guidebook, and four years later this was followed by a book, still a classic for those with direct interest, *Rock Climbing in the English Lake District*. This was written by Owen Glynne Jones, one among a number who made remarkable advances in rock climbing. In his book, he lists some seventy-five routes, grading them from 'Easy Courses' to 'Exceptionally Severe Courses'. In 1896, Jones, accompanied by the two Abraham brothers, climbed Scafell Pinnacle from Deep Ghyll, and two years later found an even more exposed line from Lord's Rake.

The Abraham brothers, George Dixon and Ashley Perry, were from Keswick and played an important part in establishing rock climbing as a sport. They were well known, of course, for their association with O.G. Jones, but were innovators in their own right. They began climbing in 1890, although their early routes were all relatively easy gullies until they teamed up with Jones in 1896. After Jones' death in 1899, the brothers continued to produce new climbs with other partners, but they were also professional photographers whose work did much to popularise climbing. They illustrated Jones' book in return for action shots of him, which they then sold from their Keswick shop.

The most popular climbing areas today are Borrowdale (Shepherd's Crag), Langdale (Gimmer Crag) and around Coniston (Dow Crag), as well as on the buttresses of Scafell and Great Gable, though climbs have been put up on almost every sizeable chunk of suitable rock throughout the Lakes. This massive expansion of the sport has been made possible by developments both in equipment and climbing techniques, and the sport, both of rock climbing and fell walking generally, has been helped along by many local education authorities that regularly bring pupils to the area for 'outdoor pursuits'.

In winter, a new dimension is added. Snow and ice have the potential to turn straightforward days out into something much more serious. And while the exponents of snow and ice climbing look forward to the coming of winter with relish, for the average walker it involves a new level of awareness and the use of additional equipment – always an ice axe, and often crampons, too, as well as extra layers of protective clothing.

What is so inspiring about the Lake District from a walker's point of view is the vast range of possibilities. At one end of the scale you can enjoy a simple stroll beside a lake or alongside a river; you can set off boldly to 'conquer' a particular summit – almost everyone sooner or later tackles Scafell Pike, the highest – or complete the round of one of the many popular 'horseshoe' walks. But there are some long distance walks, too, in and across the Lake District, that will occupy those who seek out multi-day challenges like the Cumbria Way, the Allerdale Ramble, or the intensely popular Coast to Coast Walk pioneered by Wainwright, which links St Bees on the west coast of Cumbria with Robin Hood's Bay on the other side of England, but threads a delightful course through the very heart of Lakeland on the way.

There are over 2,225 miles (3,560km) of public footpaths and bridleways in the National Park These are arguably the most important recreation resource throughout the whole of the Park and represent opportunities for visitors and residents alike to enjoy the countryside and the quality of the landscape.

The Fairfield Horseshoe, from Ambleside, is arguably the most popular of the horseshoe walks, but closely followed by the Kentmere, Langdale, Grisedale, Buttermere and Ennerdale; all long and invigorating circuits that will test the fittest and reward everyone. But there are other, equally splendid excursions. Skiddaw from Orthwaite and back via Skiddaw House is perhaps less well known than most, nor will many know the Four Passes Walk, which begins in any of the valleys encountered en route as it connects Sty Head with Black Sail, Scarth Gap and Honister.

Up Striding Edge and down Swirral Edge is always a popular route for walkers starting from Ullswater, and will (and does) test the nerve and willpower of many. Sharp Edge, too, on Blencathra, requires a good head for heights and a steady nerve, but rather less so than the ascent of Jack's Rake on Pavey Ark. This diagonal slash across the cliff face of Pavey Ark is officially graded as a moderate rock climb and has at least two key points that focus the mind for a few

The beautiful Kentmere valley attracts many walkers each year

minutes, but it is ascended almost every day during summer by walkers exploring just that little bit further.

Ironically, it is no more likely to be on intricate or demanding ascents that walkers come to grief and the mountain rescue teams called out than on straightforward walks over the fells. Accidents can happen anywhere, and tiredness overcomes everyone at some stage. Throw in the added dimension of a sudden change in the weather, and what was a simple problem to resolve can take on epic proportions. Thankfully, the mountain rescue teams of the Lake District are among the finest in Britain, ready to come to the assistance of anyone, and many of them include National Park rangers among their ranks – let's hope you never need them.

Walkers seeking solitude these days will need to know their way around the Lake District extremely well: even on a Monday at the beginning of February, in misty conditions on the remote Caldbeck Fells, I encountered eight other people – two fell runners and three couples. But there are numerous places where you can sit peacefully and enjoy the sound of silence and the companionship of solitude – I'm just not going to tell you where they are.

But recreation in the Lake District is not just about fell walking or rock climbing, the National Park offers a wide range of opportunities, and although walking is popular, so is sight-seeing, golf and sailing. Nor is it just for the visitor that recreational opportunity exists. Many facilities – football pitches, cricket pitches,

Above: A walker in Cathedral Quarry, Little Langdale

Opposite: Striding Edge in winter; no place for the inexperienced

Above: Sailing on Coniston Water with Dow Crag behind (Coniston Old Man is hidden by the sail)

Opposite: Angling on Esthwaite Water: a study in peace and tranquillity

tennis courts, sports centres and swimming pools – represent an important resource for the local communities, too.

Golf, too, is an important recreational pursuit, the popularity of which has grown significantly. There are five courses in the Lake District at Windermere, Keswick, Silecroft, Crook and Cockermouth, and a small part of the course at Kendal is within the National Park boundary. Pony trekking and equestrian centres also feature in the National Park, and are important to visitors and residents, though there is some concern about the impact they have on the landscape.

The lakes and tarns also provide recreational opportunities and pleasure for visitors. Boat launching is permitted on a number of the lakes – Windermere, Ullswater, Derwent Water, Coniston, Bassenthwaite and Thirlmere – though, at the time of writing, all except Windermere have a 10mph speed limit, which effectively excludes powerboats and jet skis. On many others, private craft are prohibited, but dinghies, canoes and rowing boats are allowed on other lakes (in some cases, for example, Esthwaite Water, where a permit is required to use a rowing boat) with restrictions – including Buttermere, Crummock Water and Grasmere.

Angling, too, remains a popular reason for visits to the Lake District, but this is a closely regulated sport and in general, permits are required by anyone wanting to fish in the lakes and rivers. The fishing rights along many of the rivers are, however, owned privately or by clubs.

6 Exploring the Park

AMBLESIDE

Ambleside is one of Lakeland's most popular tourist centres, lying in a strategic position along the first turnpike road to run through the area of the present-day National Park. It is a pleasing arrangement of slate houses, cottages, shops and hotels built in the traditional Lakeland style.

The Romans built one of their forts (*Galava*) to the south of the town at Borrans Field from where an important road ran, probably, through Troutbeck and onto the high ground of the eastern fells, bound for the fort at Brougham.

The town is essentially a large village, which received its market charter in 1650, and still holds a small market on Wednesday each week. This has always been a busy little place, of key importance to anyone exploring central Lakeland.

The intriguing Bridge House stands on what was probably a packhorse bridge spanning Stock Ghyll and is now used as a National Trust information centre. It was built in the eighteenth century and is said to have housed a family with six children. Originally, it was a summerhouse, part of the now-demolished Ambleside Hall, and has seen use as a cobbler's and an antiques shop.

Above: Bridge House, Ambleside, once housed a family with six children
Below: Ambleside from Latterbarrow

Just on the edge of Ambleside, Stockghyll Park, contains fine waterfalls that for hundreds of years provided the motive power for a wide range of mills – carding and fulling, linen, paper, corn and saw. The parish church of St Mary, however, seems rather out of keeping with the town. It was built between 1850 and 1854 in the Early Gothic style and, unlike most Lakeland churches, has a spire and makes use of sandstone, known locally as 'freestone' because of the ease with which it can be worked.

On a Saturday in July, the church holds a rush-bearing ceremony, an event depicted on a mural in the church painted in 1944 by Gordon Ransome, a student of the Royal College of Art which had been evacuated to Ambleside during the Second World War.

It is thought that rush-bearing ceremonies are a relic of Roman times, an ancient tradition kept alive in just a few Cumbrian villages (Grasmere, Great Musgrave, Urswick and Warcop are the others). The custom dates from the time when church floors, many now covered with flagstones, were strewn with another local, but less durable covering, rushes. In some churches, the bodies of parishioners were buried inside the church, and so it was important to keep the atmosphere in the church fragrant. So, it seems likely that the laying of rushes, which would have gone some way to subdue unpleasant aromas, was carried out at other times of the year, too.

The Armitt is Ambleside's own interactive exhibition of Lakeland life and times, exploring Lakeland history from the Bronze Age. The Armitt Library contains numerous books and manuscripts contributed by famous authors like Charlotte Mason, Harriet Martineau (who used to live in Ambleside), Canon Rawnsley, Collingwood, Arthur Ransome and Beatrix Potter.

South of Ambleside, on the main road, stands Brockhole, originally a large country house built for Henry Gaddum, a Manchester businessman. Later, it was used as a convalescent home, but is now the National Park's Visitor Centre, housing permanent displays and exhibitions.

Top: Brockhole, the National Park Visitor Centre
Above: Askham, an ancient and attractive village, in spring

ASKHAM

Adjoining the River Lowther on the eastern rim of the National Park, Askham is an ancient and attractive village, built around two greens. The village dates from the seventeenth century and is overlooked by the towers of Lowther Castle, built by Robert Smirke, who later constructed the British Museum and the College of Physicians in London. But the area around Askham has been inhabited since the late Stone Age; there are prehistoric settlements on nearby Skirsgill Hill, containing hut circles, and more sites at Moor Divock.

The church of St Peter, also Smirke's handiwork, was built during the reign of William IV on the site of an older church; it is one of an unusually large number of buildings of architectural or historic interest. Among these is Askham Hall, set back at the foot of the village, formerly the home of the Sandford family, but which later became, and still is, the home of the earls of Lonsdale. The fifth earl, Hugh Cecil Lonsdale (1857–1944) instituted the Lonsdale Belt for boxing and was the first president of the Automobile Association.

BACKBARROW

It was to Backbarrow that Isaac Wilkinson, father of John Wilkinson (1728–1808), the English ironmaster and inventor, moved in 1738 and developed the first iron furnaces. The village, which sits beside the River Leven at the southern end of Windermere, was the last place in England to smelt iron ore with charcoal.

In the nearby river, you can still find weirs that are relics from the days when the monks of Cartmel Priory had a flourmill here. Today, the mill is part of the Lakeland village, a timeshare complex.

Bowness flourished after the arrival of the railway

BOOTLE

Bootle is one of only four 'Cumberland' settlements to be included in the Domesday Book. Then, Cumberland did not exist; virtually the whole of Lakeland was part of Scotland, and William had to content himself with just a small foothold in this remote part of the country. They were listed, nominally, under Yorkshire!

Wordsworth had nothing praiseworthy to say of Bootle, complaining that the weather was inclement and the ocean made too much noise. But in spite of the bad press, Bootle today is a very pleasant small village of some antiquity, lying between the tumescent dome of Black Combe and the Cumbrian coast.

The right to hold a market was originally granted in 1348, by charter of Edward III, and then renewed by Elizabeth I. The church of St Michael and All Angels contains some Norman elements, but it was extensively repaired during Victorian times.

BOWNESS-ON-WINDERMERE

Like its neighbour, Windermere, Bowness flourished after the arrival of the railway, and is now a sprawling tourist town on the lake; it is from here that most of the lake cruises operate.

The village has a history extending back to the eleventh century, when the Vikings settled here and named the lake 'Vinand's Mere'. It grew only slowly, and until the railway reached Windermere was little more than a scattering of cottages and huts used by lake fishermen. But once wealthy businessmen saw the advantages of having a home away from their place of work and amid such splendid scenery, and the tourists flooded into the area, Bowness grew quickly.

The Windermere Steamboat Museum in Rayrigg Road houses a unique collection of historic steamboats and motorboats, including, it is said, the oldest mechanically powered boat in the world.

BROUGHTON-IN-FURNESS

The market town of Broughton lies at the southern edge of the National Park, where the River Duddon broadens into an estuary, and was of strategic importance during the times of the Border Troubles and much earlier.

A market charter was granted during Elizabethan times, and its importance is celebrated each year on the first day of August by the Reading of the Charter at the Market Cross, following which everyone takes refreshments at the expense of the lord of the manor, these days the county council.

The town hall dates from the eighteenth century and used to be a market hall; it now houses the tourist information office. The town square, surrounded by chestnut trees, has a set of stocks and fish slabs that are a reminder of its trading past.

To the south of the town, the church of St Mary Magdalene was consecrated in the sixteenth century, though the doorway is late Norman.

Broughton Tower and its dungeons are all that remain of the eighteenth-century mansion built by the Gilpin Sawreys around a fourteenth-century pele tower.

An annual agricultural show, a combined effort with Millom, is held during August each year.

BUTTERMERE

The name Buttermere applies not only to a delightful village, but to the whole valley and one of its two lakes. The scenery in this dale is easy on the eye and a pleasure to behold in all the seasons. John Ruskin's private secretary, W.G. Collingwood described it as 'Nature's art for art's sake'.

The village is surrounded by high fells, and as a result is a popular place with walkers, including those happy to do no more than wander around the lake. But there is more to Buttermere than scenic gems for the village is renowned for something of a scandal, which happened early in the nineteenth century. It concerns Mary, the so-called Beauty of Buttermere, daughter of the landlord of the Fish Inn. She came to the attention of a visitor to Buttermere, who presented himself as the Honourable Alexander August Hope. He wooed and later married Mary, but it was later

*Top: The rooftops of Broughton-in-Furness; an ancient market town
Above: Buttermere: 'Nature's art for art's sake'*

discovered that he was an impostor and bigamist, John Hatfield. Less than a year after his marriage to Mary, he was hanged at Carlisle not for bigamy, but for forgery. Mary, however, remarried a Caldbeck man, and lived into old age; she is buried in Caldbeck churchyard.

Not far from the village, and feeding its waters into nearby Crummock Water, Scale Force is the highest waterfall in the Lake District, and was a popular excursion among Victorian visitors, who would sail across the lake to see it.

CALDBECK

Forever associated with the flamboyant John Peel, a legend in Lake District hunting history but who, were it not for a song written by his old friend John Woodcock Graves, may well have slipped into anonymity a long time ago, Caldbeck is an attractive and peaceful village in its own right. It is an old settlement, for hundreds of years a self-contained community that used the power of hill streams, which meet at the village, to operate more than a dozen mills.

The church of St Kentigern dates from the twelfth century, but was extensively restored in the 1930s. Its graveyard, as well as accommodating John Peel, is also the last resting place of Mary, the Beauty of Buttermere.

John Peel was born in the village in 1776, one of thirteen children, who himself fathered thirteen children. His marriage, to the daughter of a wealthy farmer from Uldale, was not approved of by his in-laws-to-be, and so the couple ran away to Gretna Green, and were married there.

Brantwood – home of John Ruskin from 1872 until his death

CONISTON

The beauty of Coniston and its lake is its setting amid quiet grassy meadows, brackeny fell slopes, beech and oak woodlands, rolling moors and high fells. It is memorable in all seasons, and has attracted many people, notably Tennyson, who spent part of his honeymoon here; W.G. Collingwood, the English artist, archaeologist, and private secretary to John Ruskin, who lived at Brantwood on the shores of Coniston Water from 1872 until his death in 1900.

Brantwood, which is open to the public all year, contains numerous items associated with Ruskin, and during Ruskin's time there became an intellectual powerhouse and one of the greatest literary and artistic centres in Europe. More information about Ruskin, one of the great figures of the Victorian Age, who shunned burial in Westminster Abbey in favour of the churchyard in Coniston, is contained in the Ruskin Museum in Yewdale Road.

Another literary great, Arthur Ransome, made Coniston Water the setting for the adventures recounted in *Swallows and Amazons*.

Coniston is one of the most popular places in Lakeland, gazed down upon by craggy fells that carry the hallmarks of volcanic origin. The village properties, however, are mostly made of slate, and its prosperity grew from the quarrying of slate and the mining of copper, the latter quite possibly dating from Norman times, but mainly worked from the sixteenth century onwards.

The lake itself was the scene of Donald Campbell's ill-fated attempt at the world water-speed record on 4 January, 1967, when, as he sought to raise the record to 300mph, his jet-powered boat, *Bluebird*, went out of control. Campbell was killed and his body never recovered from the depths of the lake.

A much slower use of the lake was introduced in 1859 with the launching by the Furness Railway Company of a steam yacht, *The Gondola*, which for many years thereafter carried visitors up and down the lake, then remote and little known. Following its retirement in 1936, *The Gondola* stood unused and decaying at the southern end of the lake, until it was restored and recommissioned in 1980 by the National Trust.

To the north of Coniston is Tarn Hows, arguably the most-visited beauty spot in the Lake District and also in the care of the National Trust; it was once owned by Beatrix Potter. Here is a tranquil place for picnics and family outings set around an artificial lake constructed intentionally to enhance the landscape.

DACRE

The unpretentious village of Dacre is quite fascinating and laden with history. It is thought to have been the site of a Saxon monastery, and some authorities believe it was here that the king of England, Aethelstan, grandson of Alfred the Great, verified the Peace of Dacre with Constantine, the king of Scotland and Eugenius of Cumberland. Aethelstan was a powerful warrior king, to whom the pagan kings swore allegiance and were baptised into Christianity.

The village is set in beautiful isolation among the low fells north of Ullswater, and centres on its castle, which began life as a pele tower, built in the fourteenth century as defence against marauding Scots.

The Gondola *on Coniston Water – recommissioned by the National Trust in 1980*

The church of St Andrew boasts a Norman tower and a late twelfth-century chancel, and is believed to be on the site of that ancient monastery. At the four corners of the churchyard are the enigmatic Dacre Bears, four large stone sculptures which are thought to commemorate the marriage between Thomas de Dacre and Philippa Neville, although their true meaning is unknown.

East of Dacre stands Dalemain House, an eighteenth-century mansion built around an earlier house, and set in elegant parkland. There has been a dwelling on this site since Saxon times, and the shape of the present house – Elizabethan behind a Georgian façade – was dictated as much by domestic and agricultural demands as by the fashion of the day.

Dalemain has remained in the same family since 1679, when it was bought for £2,710 by Sir Edward Hasell who had settled in Cumberland and was secretary to Lady Anne Clifford. The house is open to the public and contains interesting pictures and furniture, and the Westmorland and Cumberland Yeomanry Museum. The sixteenth-century great barn contains examples of old agricultural machinery and a Fell Pony Museum.

ELTERWATER

Very much a setting-off place for walks into the surrounding and very beautiful landscape, Elterwater is a gathering of attractive cottages, shops and a popular pub. The name of the village is thought to mean 'Swan Lake' in Norse, and must surely be an age-old and touching reference to the occasional visits by whooper swans to nearby Elter Water during winter months.

The village used to be the centre of a thriving charcoal burning industry that used juniper wood, especially suitable, it seems, for making gunpowder. The manufacture of gunpowder, not an industry instantly associated with the Lake District, was an important source of employment, and the gunpowder works at Elter Water survived into the twentieth century.

GLENRIDDING

Originally founded on the development of the Greenside Lead Mine, Glenridding, on the shores of Ullswater, has grown into a major tourist centre, further popularised by a television drama series set there in the late 1990s. The village is one of the main starting points for ascents of Helvellyn and for boat trips on the lake.

Lead ore was first discovered in the 1650s, high in the fells above the lake, but it was another forty years before Dutch adventurers drove the first levels. Large-scale production at the mine, however, did not begin until the late eighteenth century.

Opposite: (top) The head of Ullswater and Glenridding with St Sunday Crag beyond; (below) Elter Water, Lakeland's 'Swan Lake'
Right: A wintry view of Aira Force, part of the National Trust's holdings

Grasmere seen from high on Silver How

Work at the mine continued into the 1960s, by which time it had become uneconomic to continue operations and it was closed. Most of the mine buildings are gone, but those that remain have found new life in the form of a youth hostel and mountain huts.

Between Glenridding and Pooley Bridge at the northern end of the lake, lies Gowbarrow Park, a medieval deer park containing the popular waterfall, Aira Force, now owned and cared for by the National Trust. Gowbarrow is, however, renowned for its association with Wordsworth and his poem about daffodils, which were noted and recorded by his sister, Dorothy, in her journal in 1802.

GRASMERE

The village of Grasmere, lying, as poet Thomas Gray put it, in 'the bosom of the mountains', is an attractive place regardless of the Wordsworth associations. Here, cottages, houses, shops and inns, made of gentle-hued grey-green and purple-hazed local stone, gather in a sheltered hollow, encircled by fells of varying heights and steepness. The nearby lake of Grasmere, adds a touch of class that is missing from other less endowed Lakeland villages.

Of course, you cannot escape the Wordsworth connection, though Grasmere had many bad memories and sorrow for the family. From 1799 to 1808, they lived at Dove Cottage, just off the main road, before moving to Allan Bank until 1811. Dove Cottage is open to the public, and contains many of Wordsworth's personal belongings, paintings and drawings. It was here that Wordsworth enjoyed what has become known as his 'Golden Decade', and that Dorothy wrote her *Journals*, an almost daily account of their daily lives. Allan Bank, however, is not open, nor is the rectory, where the family lived briefly before moving to Rydal Mount until his death in 1850.

Wordsworth is buried in a quiet corner of St Oswald's churchyard, along with Mary (his wife), Dorothy, and three of his children. Their graves shelter beneath one of eight yew trees that Wordsworth planted in the churchyard.

The nearby Gingerbread Shop, built in 1660, was formerly the village school, attended by the Wordsworth children during the time they lived at the rectory. Church Stile, opposite the church, is one of the oldest cottages in the village, and dates from the sixteenth century. In Wordsworth's day, it was an inn.

Each year, Grasmere, like a few other Lake District villages, holds a rush-bearing ceremony, on the first Saturday in August. The church is the focal point of the ceremony. It is a rough-hewn, pebble-dash structure on the banks of the River Rothay, and occupies a site of churches going back to Saxon times, though the oldest part of the present building is thirteenth century. Oswald was a Northumbrian king, a strong advocate of Christianity, who was killed in AD642 by a heathen king of Mercia.

Grasmere is famous, too, for its annual sports day, held in late August. The day features many local traditional sports and activities, including fell racing, Cumberland wrestling and hound trailing. An annual art exhibition is held each April, and features the work of artists living or working in Cumbria.

HAWKSHEAD

The village of Hawkshead has flourished since Norse times, and later expanded as it became the place where a number of packhorse trails that were developed to link the Windermere ferries with the Coniston valley, met. It is an attractive village, and popular for a number of reasons, not least the fact that Wordsworth was educated here from 1779–1787.

But the focal point, as in any market town, is the market place, which sits in the middle of a snug arrangement of limewashed cottages, narrow streets, squares and cobbled pavements, from which low archways lead to concealed courtyards, most of which is pedestrianised and greatly enhanced as a result.

The Beatrix Potter Gallery, next to the Red Lion pub, is housed in rooms formerly occupied by local solicitor, William Heelis, who married Beatrix Potter. The gallery, now owned by the National Trust, houses a changing exhibition of Beatrix Potter's sketches and watercolours.

Also part of the National Trust's holdings is Hawkshead Courthouse at the

Hawkshead began life as a Norse settlement

junction of the Ambleside and Coniston roads, half a mile north of Hawkshead. This is all that remains of a medieval grange used by the monks of Furness Abbey to administer their estates. Manorial courts used to be held in the large upper room.

The village church, dedicated to St Michael, occupies an elevated position on a grassy hillock above the school. It dates from the sixteenth and seventeenth centuries.

KENDAL

The market town of Kendal is not within the National Park, but is the seat of the National Park authority's administrative offices. It is a major tourist town, in close proximity to the Lake District, and the largest town in the now defunct county of Westmorland.

The main thoroughfare is Highgate, from which flows a series of courtyards, many of them named and numbered and thought to have been part of a defensive system typical of towns that were under constant threat from Scottish marauders.

The town was granted a market charter in 1189, and since 1989 commemorates the event by holding an entertaining medieval market when all the stallholders and a few roaming jesters dress in period costume.

Kendal occupies a position on the River Kent strategically important enough for the Romans to have wanted a fort (*Alauna*) here, though there is little evidence of it today.

The fame of the town grew during the sixteenth century when Kendal bowmen clad in Kendal Green cloth fought at the Battle of Flodden Field. Later descriptions relate how men and women were to be seen knitting stockings as they went about their business in the town.

Just outside the town is Kendal Castle, thought to date from the twelfth century, and home to the barons of Kendal. In the sixteenth century, it was owned by Sir Thomas Parr, father of Catherine Parr, and the last wife of Henry VIII, who was born in the castle in 1512.

Kendal church – dedicated to the Holy and Undivided Trinity – is the county's largest church, and dates from the thirteenth century, though most of the present massive edifice is Victorian restoration.

The Abbot Hall Museum of Lakeland Life and Industry displays traditional rural trades, and illustrates how Cumbrian people lived and worked. Abbot Hall Gallery in Kirkland, is an imposing Georgian house accommodating an art gallery with acclaimed exhibition programmes. Kendal Museum of Natural History and Archaeology in Station Road, is one of the oldest museums in the country, and depicts developments from prehistoric times to the twentieth century.

Forever associated with his pocket guidebooks to the Lakeland fells, Alfred Wainwright lived in Kendal for fifty years until his

Skiddaw from Surprise View, above Derwent Water

death in 1991, and for some time was the town's Borough Treasurer. His office in the town hall is now used as the tourist information centre.

KESWICK

The town of Keswick is the largest in the National Park, and expanded considerably during Elizabethan times when it was an important mining centre. For most visitors, however, Keswick is an attractive town splendidly positioned between two important lakes and at the foot of one of Lakeland's most popular mountains, Skiddaw.

In spite of its undoubted antiquity, Keswick is largely a Victorian town that flourished after the coming of the railway that linked Penrith and Cockermouth. The town, built from local stone, blends wonderfully well with the surrounding landscape, and is always a pleasure to visit.

Keswick's agricultural show, which includes the Cumbrian Champion Sheepdog Trials, is held at the end of August on the showground at Crossings Field.

Barrow Bay, Derwent Water

The Keswick Museum and Art Gallery in Fitz Park is a Victorian museum that has a fine local history collection dating from Roman times.

Of much older vintage is the Castlerigg stone circle on the fells to the south-east of the town. It is believed to dated from 3000BC, which makes it older than Stonehenge, and it is considered to be the most superb stone circle in the country and among the earliest in Europe.

NEAR SAWREY

Near Sawrey is one of two villages, the other is Far Sawrey, that lie amid a rolling, wooded landscape of considerable beauty between Windermere and Esthwaite Water.

Near Sawrey is renowned for its association with writer Beatrix Potter. In 1905, she bought Hill Top Farm (now owned by the National Trust) and, though it was never her permanent residence, she created here the world of Jemima Puddle-Duck, Tom Kitten and Pigling Bland, and in so doing delighted countless generations of young and old alike.

PATTERDALE

The dale we call Patterdale is named after St Patrick, who, along with St Ninian and St Kentigern, travelled throughout this part of the Lake District on evangelical missions in the early part of the fifth century. The village is an elongated affair at the southern end of Ullswater, catering largely for walkers and day-trippers.

The village church is, perhaps predictably, dedicated to St Patrick, and was largely rebuilt in 1853.

The annual Dog Day at the end of August is a traditional show with sheepdog trials, sheep shearing, hound trailing and rural crafts.

POOLEY BRIDGE

Both the main streets in Pooley Bridge are lined with charming stone houses and cottages. The village spans the River Eamont, formerly the boundary between Cumberland and Westmorland, and lies at the northern end of Ullswater. There are tremendous views down the lake from the village, which now caters mainly for tourists. But Pooley Bridge used to be a busy place with a regular market, including a fish market and a sheep and cattle fair, though it was always overshadowed by the market in nearby Penrith.

Before the bridge was built in the sixteenth century, the village was simply known as 'Pooley', from 'a pool by the hill'. The hill here is Dunmallet, which has a small Iron Age fort on its summit.

RYDAL

There is little substance to the village of Rydal, a scattered grey-stone community along the turnpike between Ambleside and Keswick, but it remains extremely popular with tourists who come to visit Rydal Mount, where the Wordsworth family lived, having moved from Grasmere in 1813. This was a social step up for Wordsworth, which put him on calling terms with the local gentry. He lived here until his death, though his best work had all been accomplished, mainly at Dove Cottage in Grasmere.

Not far away is Nab Cottage, an early eighteenth-century farmhouse, where poet Thomas de Quincey spent much of his time courting Margaret (Peggy) Simpson, whom he later married. Another writer, Hartley Coleridge, eldest son of Samuel Taylor Coleridge, spent his last eleven years at Nab Cottage. He was seriously addicted to drink, and would often disappear into the fells on drinking sprees.

Top: Near Sawrey, popular with Beatrix Potter fans
Above: Rydal Mount – Wordsworth's last home

Nearby, and below Rydal Mount, Rydal Hall has an early Victorian front that conceals a seventeenth-century house lived in by the le Flemings, once the major local landowners. Rydal Park, close by, is the scene of the Rydal Sheepdog Trials, held each August.

STAVELEY

Now bypassed by Lakeland-bound traffic, Staveley is a mainly residential village of grey-slate cottages and houses between the River Gowan and the River Kent.

The area around Staveley has been inhabited since about 4000BC, when the countryside was populated by Celtic-speaking British farmers.

Staveley was granted a market charter in the thirteenth century, but vastly expanded at the time of the Industrial Revolution. As transport improved, the village became the bobbin-turning capital of Westmorland. It is still a small industrial village, with a fascinating history.

THRELKELD

The story of the village of Threlkeld, tucked in neatly below the steep slopes of Blencathra, goes back more than 800 years. Its name is derived from the Norse and means 'the well of the thrall' – a thrall being a medieval term for a man bound in service. There seems to have been a settlement in the locality during the Dark Ages,

The bold form of Blencathra is a challenge to every walker

and possibly from Roman times. By the thirteenth century, it was large enough to have its own priest, though the present church of St Mary dates from 1777.

Today, the village is bypassed by the main road and sits along the old road that in days gone by would have resounded to trains of packhorses, cattle and sheep droves, as well as a regular stagecoach service, for this was a busy place. The Horse and Farrier Inn, which dates from 1688, is a reminder of those past times.

The village is, of course, dominated by the swelling bulk of Blencathra, an immensely popular fell with more than half a dozen ways to its summit.

The Threlkeld Quarry and Mining Museum contains a fine collection of original artefacts, plans and other mining and quarrying memorabilia, and includes a display of minerals and geological specimens.

Each year in August, the village holds sheepdog trials on Burns Recreation Field, a popular event that includes foxhound and terrier shows and hound trailing.

WINDERMERE

The village of Windermere, half a mile from the lake of the same name, used to be called Birthwaite, but when the Kendal and Windermere Railway opened in

1847, and the station built at Birthwaite, the name was considered to be uninspiring and was changed.

The railway, of course, was instrumental in developing Windermere, which happened rather quickly as it became popular with commuting industrialists, many of whom built the large houses that are a major feature of the town.

Windermere, the lake, is the largest in England, being 10½ miles (17km) long and 1 mile (1.6km) wide at its broadest. The shores of the lake are wooded throughout much of its length, high ground overlooks it, and islands punctuate the waters, in the case of Belle Isle almost cutting it in two. Inevitably, for many years the lake served as an important highway. The Romans imported stone to build their fort at Ambleside, and later the lake was used to transport iron ore to a number of smelting furnaces that developed along the lakeshore and made extensive use of the plentiful supply of wood for charcoal.

The lake is renowned for char, which in its potted form was a considerable delicacy among the wealthy families of the seventeenth and eighteenth centuries.

By the middle of the nineteenth century, however, Windermere had begun to serve a less utilitarian function and saw the growth of pleasure sailing which has now become the principal activity on the lake.

Overleaf: Windermere and Wetherlam from Waterhead, Ambleside

Below: Belle Isle, Windermere and Bowness from Low Pate Crag

Information

USEFUL ADDRESSES

Lake District National Park
Authority, Murley Moss,
Oxenholme Road, Kendal, Cumbria
LA9 7RL
Tel: 01539 724555
Fax: 01539 740822
Email: hq@lake-district.gov.uk
Web-site: www.lake-district.gov.uk
Camping barn bookings,
Moot Hall, Keswick
Tel: 017687 72645

Cumbria Tourist Board, Ashleigh,
Holly Road, Windermere, Cumbria
LA23 2AQ
Tel: 015394 44444
Fax: 015394 44041
Email: mail@cumbria-tourist-
board.co.uk
Web-site: www.cumbria-the-lake-
district.co.uk

Cumbria Wildlife Trust, Brockhole,
Windermere,
Cumbria LA23 1LJ
Tel: 015394 48280
Fax: 015394 48281

English Heritage
Head Office: 23 Savile Row, London
W1X 1AB
Tel: 0171 973 3250.
Fax: 0171 973 3146
Web-site: www.english-
heritage.org.uk
Regional office: Bessie Surtees
House, 41–44 Sandhill, Newcastle-
upon-Tyne NE1 3JF
Tel: 0191 269 1227
Fax: 0191 261 1130

English Nature, Juniper House,
Murley Moss, Oxenholme Road,
Kendal, Cumbria LA9 7RL
Tel: 01539 792800

Fax: 01539 792830
Email: Cumbria@english-
nature.org.uk

Forestry Enterprise, Lakes Forest
District, Grizedale, Hawkshead,
Ambleside, Cumbria LA22 0QJ
Tel: 01229 860373
Fax: 01229 860273

Friends of the Lake District,
No 3, Yard 77, Highgate, Kendal,
Cumbria LA9 4ED
Tel/Fax: 01539 720788

Lake District Visitor Centre at
Brockhole, Windermere,
Cumbria LA23 1LJ
Tel: 015394 46601

National Trust
Regional Office: The Hollens,
Grasmere, Ambleside,

Opposite: Kirkstone Pass, looking towards Brotherswater
Right: Herdwick sheep
Overleaf: Interlocking spurs in Skiddaw Slates are carved by Sail Beck, Buttermere

Cumbria LA22 9QZ
Tel: 015394 35599
Fax: 01539 435353
Town Shop: Grasmere Information
Centre and Shop, Chapel Stile,
Grasmere (Tel: 015394 35621)

Weatherline: 017687 75757

Youth Hostels Association
Head Office: Trevelyan House,
8 St Stephen's Hill,
St Albans,
Herts. AL1 2DY.
Tel: 01727 855215
General enquiries:
Tel: 01727 845047 or email:
customerservices@yha.org.uk
Lake District bookings: Contact
Ambleside Youth Hostel,
Waterhead,
Ambleside,
Cumbria LA22 0EU
Tel: 015394 32304
Fax: 015394 34408
Email: ambleside@yha.org.uk

Major attractions
Steam Yacht *Gondola*,
　Coniston Water
　Tel: 015394 36003
Beatrix Potter Gallery,
　Hawkshead
　Tel: 015394 36355
Hill Top,
　Near Sawrey
　Tel: 015394 36269
Ullswater Steamers
　Tel: 017684 82229
　Townend, Troutbeck
　Tel: 015394 32628
Cumberland Derwent Pencil
　Museum
　Tel: 017687 73626
Lakeside and Haverthwaite
　Railway
　Tel: 015395 31594
The Armitt Museum,
　Ambleside
　Tel: 015394 31212

The Ruskin Museum,
　Coniston
　Tel: 015394 41164
Windermere Lake Cruises,
　Bowness
　Tel: 015394 43360
Dove Cottage and Wordsworth
　Museum,
　Grasmere
　Tel: 015394 35544
Ravenglass and Eskdale Railway
　Tel: 01229 717171
Aquarium of the Lakes,
　Newby Bridge
　Tel: 015395 30153
World of Beatrix Potter Attraction,
Windermere
　Tel: 015394 88444

MAPS

The use of excellent appropriate
Ordnance Survey maps is highly
recommended for any detailed
exploration of the National Park,
especially if you are leaving the car
behind and venturing out into the
countryside.

Outdoor Leisure Maps (1:25,000)
No 4 English Lakes – North
Western area;
No 5 English Lakes – North
Eastern area;
No 6 English Lakes – South
Western area;
No 7 English Lakes – South Eastern
area

FURTHER READING

Fisher, Andrew. *A Traveller's History
of Scotland* (Windrush Press, 2nd
ed. 1997)
Hunt, Irvine (ed). *Norman Nicholson's
Lakeland: A Prose Anthology*
(Robert Hale, 1991)
Lake District National Park Local
Plan (Lake District National Park
Authority, 1998)
Lefebure, Molly. *Cumbrian Discovery*
(Victor Gollancz, 1977)
The Illustrated Lake Poets (Tiger
Books International, 1992)
Lindop, Grevel. *A Literary Guide to
the Lake District* (Chatto and
Windus, 1993)
Marsh, Terry. *Towns and Villages of
Cumbria* (Sigma Press, 1998)
Millward, Roy and Robinson,
Adrian. *The Lake District* (Eyre
and Spottiswood, 1970)
Moorman, Mary (ed). *Journals of
Dorothy Wordsworth* (Oxford
Paperbacks, 1971)
Nicholson, Norman. *The Lakers: The
First Tourists* (Robert Hale, 1955)
Portrait of the Lakes (Robert Hale,
1963)
Rice, H. A. L., *Lake Country Echoes*
(Westmorland Gazette, 1973)
Lake Country Portraits (Harvill Press,
1967)
Rollinson, William. *A History of
Cumberland and Westmorland*
(Phillimore, 1978)
Rowling, Marjorie. *The Folklore of
the Lake District* (B.T. Batsford,
1976)
Selincourt, Ernest de (ed).
Wordsworth's Guide to the Lakes
(Oxford University Press, 1906)

Index

Page numbers in *italics* indicate illustrations